A NEW TEACHING, A

...ᴜ

A Guide to Teachin᷎   ᴜɪogy

TEF Study Guides

This series was first sponsored and subsidized by the Theological Education Fund of the WCC in response to requests from Africa, Asia, the Caribbean, and the Pacific. The books are prepared by and in consultation with theological teachers in those areas. Special attention is given to problems of interpretation and application arising there as well as in the West, and to the particular needs of students using English as a second language. More advanced titles in the list are marked (A).

General Editors: Daphne Terry and Nicholas Beddow

TEF Guide 25 (ADVANCED)

A NEW TEACHING, A NEW LEARNING

A Guide to Teaching Theology

Gerald Collier

First published in Great Britain 1989
SPCK
Holy Trinity Church
Marylebone Road
London NW1 4DU

Thanks are due to the following for permission to reproduce copyright material: Darton, Longman
& Todd for the extract from *Praying the Kingdom* by Charles Elliott (1985); Heinemann Publishing
Ltd for the extract from *The River Between* by Ngugi Wa Thiong'o (1965); and The Society of
Authors on behalf of the Bernard Shaw Estate for the extract from *Saint Joan*.

British Library Cataloguing in Publication Data

Collier, Gerald
  A new technology, a new learning.—(TEF study guide; 25).
  1. Education. Curriculum subjects. Theology. Teaching
  I. Title II. Series
  230'.07

ISBN 0-281-04365-5

Typeset and printed in Great Britain by
Latimer Trend & Company Ltd, Plymouth

To Gwen

Contents

CONTENTS

Preface

I have received generous help from a great many people in preparing this book. I am especially indebted to the following:

The Rev. Graham Kings of St Andrew's Institute, Kabare, Kenya, for his highly efficient organization of my Kenyan tour and his many detailed and shrewd comments on the first draft of the book; and also to him and his wife Ali for their generous hospitality to my wife and myself during our two visits to Kabare.

The Revs. Agustin and Rosario Batlle, the Rev. Dr Kiranga Gatimu and Deaconess Margaret Thornton for precious discussions on the development of TEE work in Africa; for the opportunity of sitting in on four TEE classes in the diocese of Nakuru, Kenya; for many valuable comments on the first draft of this book; and for the opportunity of working through some of the new workbooks now being prepared.

The Rev. Ian Bunting, Professor Jimmy Dunn, Canon Professor Dan Hardy, the Rev. Dr Willy Morrice and Dr Robert Smith for expert comments on my first draft and for valuable advice on reading and on the management of the Durham University word processors.

The Rt Rev. David Gitari, Bishop of Mount Kenya East, Kenya, for consistent interest and encouragement for the project.

Dr Jesse Mugambi for many useful comments on the project.

Pam Wilding for much help in the typing of documents.

The Rev. Enos and Gertrude Ashimala, the Rev. Peter Ensor, the Rev. Mark and Anna Russell-Smith, the Rev. Joseph and Jenifer Wasonga, Dr Peter and Hannah Williams and the Rev. William Wesa for their warm welcome and hospitable arrangements in their respective colleges in Kenya.

The Rev. Mark and Sally Ashcroft, the Rev. Johannes and Mrs Beks, the Rev. Dr Charles and Gaby Hein, the Rev. Edward Karani, Deaconess Joyce Karuri, the Rev. Grant and Wendy le Marquand, the Rev. John Mbogo, Deaconess Esther Mombo, the Rev. Moses Mwangi, the Rev. John Odaga, Canon Dick and the Rev. Linda Tyree, the Rev. Francis and Elaine Wainaina, and the Rev. Dr and Mrs Boo Woong Yoo for allowing me to attend their classes and give me interviews, as well as, in many cases, for delightful hospitality.

The Rev. Nick Beddow, General Editor of the TEF series of Study Guides for SPCK, for consistently enthusiastic support in the project and for setting up my visit to Kenya. It was Nick Beddow's idea to enlist an educationist rather than a theologian to work out a range of principles and techniques on the organizing of students' learning in theology, and to check these against the realities and practical problems of the practitioners in a developing country, and I have found the whole enterprise immensely rewarding.

Daphne Terry for her most thorough reviewing of my text and her many penetrating and sensitive comments and suggestions on it.

Despite all the friendly guidance I have received, I have no doubt that the thinness of my theological knowledge will be quickly apparent to any reader with a theological training: the faults in the text are my responsibility alone. I can only offer a modest prayer that, in compensation, what I have written about ways of guiding students' learning may make some small contribution to a wider understanding of the gospel and a deeper commitment to the Christian faith.

GERALD COLLIER

1

The aims and organization of this book

ARRANGEMENT OF THE MATERIAL

In writing this book I have had two main sets of readers in mind. First, there are tutors who are engaged in 'Theological Education by Extension' (TEE) work; and second, there are those who are engaged in full-time theological education in universities, seminaries, theological colleges and Bible Schools. But I hope it will also be of use to the many clergy, pastors and lay Christians who are involved in systematic teaching of one sort or another.

Part 1 of the book is a general outline of the aims and purposes involved in theological education for adult students, whether they are taking part in an extension programme or in a college or university. The five chapters in this section set out eleven key objectives which represent, in a summary form, what many of those who train Church leaders would regard as crucial in the development of a balanced education involving both the heart and the head.

Most TEE programmes are designed for people who live far from a college and have to do much of their study in isolation. However, regular meetings of such home-based students with a tutor are built into the course, usually once a week; these are the Group Tutorials. TEE programmes are designed for various levels of educational background, and I have made a broad distinction between courses aimed at adults with only primary, or partial primary, schooling, and those designed for individuals who have gone through at least a large part of a secondary education. The former I refer to as 'post-primary' and the latter as 'post-secondary' or tertiary. Part 2 of the book is mainly addressed to those engaged in TEE work.

Much of Part 2 will also be useful to tutors engaged in full-time theological education, particularly perhaps chapter 10 on practical projects such as work placements, chapter 12 on tutorial work, and chapter 13 on the handling of group discussions. However, certain ways of organizing students' learning are not applicable in a TEE course, and these are taken up in chapter14 on lecturing, and chapter 15 on a particular form of small-group work known as a 'syndicate' method. These two chapters make up Part 3 of the book.

Parts 2 and 3, then, compose what may be called the basic routines of TEE and full-time college work. Not that there is a sharp dividing line to be drawn between these two, but rather a trend towards convergence. However, there is another area of training which is important for anyone engaged in theological education in the modern world: helping students to gain some insight into other cultures as well as into their own, and into themselves. Part 4 contains two chapters, 16 and 17, on these aspects.

Furthermore, since the focus of students' efforts is inevitably on the examinations they have to take, I have provided two chapters on methods of assessment: chapter 18 on the assessment of academic attainments and chapter 19 on the assessment of professional qualities. These form Part 5.

(Readers may be glad to know that a cassette is available which illustrates some of the techniques described in chapters 14 and 15. One side shows the ordering of the subject matter in a set of lectures; the other demonstrates how some of the small-group techniques can be applied. An accompanying leaflet outlines the contents of the cassette and fills in some of the details. The presenters are the author of this book, Gerald Collier, and Peter Glew, a lecturer in the Schools of Education of Durham University and Sunderland Polytechnic, who has considerable experience of syndicate work. Challenging them are the Reverend Nick Beddow, Editor of the TEF Study Guide series and a Founder Member of TEE in Zambia; the Reverend Monrelle Williams, lecturer at Codrington Theological College, Barbados; and Mrs Shaku Char, who holds an MA of the University of Madras and who has had experience of teaching in universities and schools in India and Britain. The cassette may be purchased from Gerald Collier, 4 Robson Terrace, Shincliffe, Durham DH1 2NL, UK, for the equivalent of £3 post paid.)

PRESENTATION OF THE MATERIAL

In the greater part of this book I have been faced with trying to convey practical techniques without being able to demonstrate them in person. I have therefore adopted a style of presentation which will to some extent follow in practice the principles I describe for use with students. In effect the whole book is prepared as a TEE workbook, and I hope that tutors will find this structure useful as a practical tool, whether in a college or a TEE organization. The text is developed in fairly short chapters or units of study, each divided into sections as would be the case in a workbook; and many of the sections are followed by an 'Activity': something for you as reader to *do*. Sometimes the Activity is concerned with new words or concepts introduced. Sometimes it is a 'Stop, Think and Note' exercise inviting you to check what you have just been reading against your own experience or established views. Sometimes it is a 'Research and Discussion' exercise designed to prompt you to apply in another context something you have been reading here. In all cases you will find it useful to put down your responses on paper. This can be an aid to clear thinking, and help you to put into words what you may not have had occasion to express systematically before. Where appropriate there are notes on these Activities at the end of the chapter, indicating the responses I would have expected. Some of these notes will be very wide of the mark: your circumstances and experience may well have been entirely different from what I have guessed. But whether my own comments are helpful or not, it would always be useful to talk over your responses with a friend or a colleague. All these Activities for you to carry out as you go along, and also the notes on them, are clearly distinguished from the rest of the text by means of an enclosing 'box'. Examples of actual teaching material (case studies, suggested checklists and guidelines for students, and units of various sorts from existing work books and study guides) are numbered serially throughout and distinguished by means of a vertical rule at left of the page.

In many chapters I begin by quoting fragments of recorded experience. These are intended to give a sense of the practical issues involved, and to stimulate thought on the topic about to be discussed. This technique is one which may be useful in preparing self-study materials for students. Full details of the sources of the quotations are given in the list of Further Reading (pp. 158–164), to which the numbers in parentheses given for these and other quoted materials refer. In chapters 2–6, which set the scene, in broad social and educational terms, for the detailed accounts of practical methods in chapters 7–19, I have also felt that a brief summary of the chapter may be helpful.

SCOPE OF THE MATERIAL

At this point I wish to make clear that the scope of the book is limited in two important respects.

In the first place, most individual tutors and college staffs will almost certainly have a twelfth objective in mind in conducting their courses, namely to help students to develop a depth of commitment, a conviction of the reality of God's love, and a continuing growth towards a deeply felt trust in Jesus. But a purpose of this nature cannot properly be treated by the methods that I will be describing for achieving academic and professional objectives. The critical factor in attaining this twelfth aim will be the strength of that commitment, conviction and trust in the people who do the teaching: the staff of a college, the Group Leaders of a TEE course. These convictions are communicated through a multitude of subtle and delicate ways of expressing one's deeper beliefs and feelings. For example, I myself may talk in quite glowing terms about the reality of God's love, even though I may not in fact feel this as an ever-present power. And I know that anybody I am talking to will recognize from the tone of my voice, the words I use, the expression on my face, that my *claim* to that conviction goes a long way beyond the *reality* of the conviction. To speak about it is not the same as to feel it in my bones. This sense of 'feeling something in one's bones' is what I shall mean when I speak of something as having an 'existential' reality.

The head of an institution in particular has a great influence on the way both staff and students develop in their Christian discipleship. The Book of Ecclesiasticus, in the Wisdom Literature of the Apocrypha, has expressed this well:

Like the magistrate of the people
so are his officials;
and like the ruler of the city
so are all its inhabitants. (Ecclus. 10.2)

And of course individuals in a more junior position may also have great gifts of spiritual insight. We need to think in terms of the concept of the '*koinonia*': the community or fellowship, in which a certain quality of shared living and personal relationships has grown out of a deep Christian commitment.

The same is true of people attending TEE classes: a major influence on their inner life of prayer and discipleship will be the 'inner felt beliefs and values' of the Directors or Co-ordinators of the courses, the Group Leaders and the other members of the groups.

In the second place I must make clear that I am not trying to preach a new orthodoxy of teaching. The way tutors or college staffs carry out their teaching duties depends on their objectives, and on the priorities they assign among those objectives. In chapters 2–6 I have set out eleven objectives which I regard as important, and which are commonly claimed by teachers in tertiary education. If an individual tutor, or a member of a staff team, attaches highest priority to the objective of inculcating a basic knowledge of facts, concepts, techniques and accepted views in a subject, then that will determine the form of assessment, the nature of the teaching given and the focus of the students' efforts. One may place that objective first from deep conviction, or because one attaches overriding importance to the students' success in examinations of a traditional type. Or it may be because one has simply accepted traditional assumptions without seriously questioning them, or because the prevailing culture demands that this objective be given top priority; or for some other reason. *The crucial factor is the balance of priorities in the tutor's mind or in the thinking of the staff team.* If I myself have any 'orthodoxy' to preach, it is to urge any staff tutor or team *to examine and articulate the real, felt convictions or values which underlie their actual practice.* This may be a long and arduous task, even a spiritual exercise, and there may be external constraints to be taken into account. But the only people who can carry it out are tutors themselves; it is not a job which this book can do for them.

2

Traditional aims and traditional shortfalls

SOME COMMENTS ON TRADITIONAL STYLES OF TERTIARY EDUCATION

... The degeneration of algebra into gibberish ... affords a pathetic instance of the uselessness of reforming educational schedules without a clear conception of the attributes [or qualities] which you wish to evoke in the living minds of the [pupils]. *A. N. Whitehead* (5)

... In my own work at universities I have been much struck by the paralysis of thought induced in pupils by the aimless accumulation of precise knowledge, inert and unutilized. (5)

... First-hand knowledge is the ultimate basis of intellectual life. To a large extent book-learning conveys second-hand information ... the second-handedness of the learned world is the secret of its mediocrity. It is tame because it has never been scared by facts. (5)

... The enlargement [of the mind] consists, not merely in the passive reception into the mind of a number of ideas hitherto unknown to it, but in the mind's energetic and simultaneous action upon and towards and among those new ideas ... it is a making the objects of our knowledge subjectively our own, or ... it is a digestion of what we receive, into the substance of our previous state of thought. It is an acquired illumination, a personal possession, and an inward endowment. *John Henry Newman* (6)

... Those earnest but ill-used persons who are forced to load their minds with a score of subjects against an examination, who have too much on their hands to indulge themselves in thinking or investigation, who devour premiss and conclusion together with indiscriminate greediness ... who too often, as might be expected, when their period of education is passed, throw up all they have learned in disgust. (6)

TRADITIONAL OBJECTIVES IN TERTIARY EDUCATION

Most tutors in post-school education probably intend that their students will attain something of the following objectives:

Objective 1. To acquire a reasonable command of the basic facts, concepts, techniques and accepted views in the subjects studied; i.e. to have this material well established in the memory: in short, **basic knowledge.**

Objective 2. To gain a good understanding or grasp of the subjects studied. There are three aspects here.

(a) Students should acquire a *framework of ideas* or structure of concepts, in which the facts, etc. listed in Objective 1 have a logical place. For example, in studying the concept of 'ministry' students need to have a clear idea of (among other things) the meaning of the word 'minister'; of the emphasis Jesus placed on *His* serving the disciples rather than on *their* serving *Him*; of the dilemma Jesus presented when He agreed that He was in fact the disciples' teacher and leader and yet was there to serve them; and of the problem presented to any Christian in a position of authority, as to how to combine being in authority with being a servant. There are four fairly complex concepts here to be grasped and built into a logical structure or framework of ideas.

(b) Students should acquire *the ways of thinking* and *of using evidence* that characterize the subjects studied. For example, in studying the Bible students need to learn how to interpret the audience or readership envisaged by the writers, the historical circumstances of the time, the way the stories are told, the heart of the message conveyed, the uncertainties involved in translation. This sort of thinking is quite different from that needed for the study of (say) physics. It involves using a different kind of evidence and arriving at a different kind of conclusion.

(c) Students should develop some skill in *applying these ways of thinking in settings directly comparable to those in which they were learned.* For example, a student who has worked on one of St Paul's letters should know how to set about a study of another of his letters: what questions to ask, what problems there are likely to be in interpreting the argument, etc.

These three aspects constitute a *subject discipline*: the characteristic structure of concepts and modes of argument of that subject area. We shall accordingly refer to this objective as **comprehension of the subject discipline**.

Acitivity 1: Stop, think and note Look back at your own schooling. How far did your teachers' emphasis lie with memorizing information: for example, learning by heart the names and dates of important people, or the basic facts of historical events? How far would you say you *understood* what you were memorizing? How did your teachers get you to understand what you were studying?

Objective 3. To acquire a habit, and an expectation, of learning for themselves; that is, to become sufficiently committed to their studies to be able to work effectively on their own without pressure from tutors or the prospect (or threat!) of an examination. This implies that they not only are able to work out their own views without depending on their tutors to tell them what to think, but form a lifelong habit and expectation of using books and other sources as nourishment for working out their own views. In short, they should develop a habit of autonomous or **self-directed learning.**

Objective 4. To acquire some skill in expressing ideas or feelings, reporting events, recording observations, etc.: in writing, in speech, in mathematical symbols, in pictures and/or in other media. In short, to acquire appropriate **communication skills.**

Objective 5. To acquire a capacity for applying the learned material in entirely new situations. Under Objective 2(c) the new task was fairly similar to the old: applying to a second letter of St Paul the principles of interpretation learned from a first. To apply these principles *in an entirely new situation* the task might be to study a Pastoral Letter issued by the present Pope during one of his visits to Latin America. This skill can conveniently be referred to as the application of learned material in fresh situations: in short, **application in new situations.**

Activity 2: Stop, think and note Some examination questions set problems which are very close to those given during the course (as under objective 2(c). Some on the other hand set problems quite unlike anything encountered in the course, but which can be handled by using some of the material learned (as under Objective 5). Give an example of each type of question, *either* from your own memory of exams *or* from actual examination papers *or* from a book *or* from your own devising.

Objective 6. To acquire a capacity for analysing an argument, for example in an article in the press, an interview on television, a passage in a book; that is, for identifying the different components of the communication, making clear the relationships between them and showing the structure of the argument: in short, **analysing an argument.**

Objective 7. To acquire some skill in devising new concepts, inventing new schemes, producing new plans for action, creating new works of imagination; that is, developing some inventive or creative talent in some area of activity: in short, **invention.**

Objective 8. To acquire some skill in assessing the quality of what one has learned or studied: for example, the logical sequence of an argument, the appropriateness of a solution for a problem, the relevance of a discussion to the topic under review, the efficiency or economy of a practical plan for achieving a particular end. 'Assessing the quality' is here intended to involve specifying the *criteria* or standards by which one is judging, that is, not simply expressing an *opinion* but forming a *judgement* based on a consideration of all the relevant factors. For convenience I will refer to this as **assessing quality.**

Activity 3: Stop, think and note Look back at your last year at school again. Select a subject of study which you enjoyed and a subject which you disliked. List objectives 1–8 above, and for each objective note what your teachers did to promote that objective, first in the subject you liked and, second, in the subject you disliked.

TRADITIONAL SHORTFALLS IN TERTIARY EDUCATION

The first two objectives—knowledge of basic material and compre-hension of the subject discipline—cover the routine 'didactic' courses of much tertiary education, that is, the customary lecturing and instruction in which the dominant assumption is that somebody who *knows* gives information or knowledge to somebody who does *not know*. These are 'knowledge-based' objectives. Objectives 5 (applica-tion in new situations), 6 (analysing an argument), 7 (invention) and 8 (assessing quality) are sometimes grouped together under the heading of 'higher order skills'; objectives 6 and 8 may be considered together under some such phrase as 'powers of critical judgement'. These objectives are all concerned with the processes of thinking and the skills of argument, rather than with the acquisition of knowledge, and are therefore known as 'process-based' objectives.

Activity 4: Words The word 'didactic' often implies an authoritar-ian attitude on the part of the tutor. Have any or many of the courses you have attended been rightly called 'didactic'?

Activity 5: Words Explain in your own words the meaning of the phrases 'knowledge-based objectives' and 'process-based objec-tives'.

Habits and expectations vary enormously from one country to another, and from one institution to another. In some places Objec-tives 1 and 2 cover the full extent of normal teaching practice. In some places tutors aim seriously and conscientiously at developing the higher order skills of Objectives 5, 6, 7 and 8, or perhaps just the critical judgement of Objectives 6 and 8, but in practice place so much emphasis on Objectives 1 and 2 as to make the more ambitious aims impossible to achieve. This may be because they insist on students committing to memory such a mass of undigested information that they cannot make sense of it, or even reject it all. There must be a multitude of men and women with degrees in all subjects who have said on emerging from their final examination, 'Now I can forget all that.' As a Kenyan tutor said, 'In those subjects where I was instructed and instructed and instructed, yes, I learned the facts all right for the examination, but then immediately after the examination they are forgotten.' And the staff of one university department, making a detailed analysis of final examination papers, were horrified to find that the way in which the questions were formulated compelled students to concentrate almost exclusively on Objectives 1 and 2, and prevented them from giving time to the higher order skills.

Many readers of this book must have echoed the students in a well-known medical school who simply 'found out what the staff wanted them to know' and dedicated their efforts to that one goal in order to pass their examinations: yet on entry their professors had insisted that the real aim was to develop their powers of critical judgement. Sadly, there is evidence that many TEE courses in different parts of the world focus largely on the memorization of a fixed body of information.

Activity 6: Stop, think and note 'Find out what the staff want you to know and learn it.' Have you yourself been in a school or college where this was the prevailing attitude among the students or pupils? If so, briefly describe the circumstances.

As they stand, the higher order skills contained in Objectives 5, 6, 7 and 8, though sadly neglected in practice, are in themselves straightforward and uncontroversial. But they are so broad and abstract as to offer little practical guidance, and we need to turn to recent research on student learning and on training for the professions to find practical assistance in the planning of courses.

SUMMARY

The main part of the chapter describes eight Objectives which would probably be agreed by many teachers in higher education, which in headline form are:
   1. **Basic knowledge**
   2. **Comprehension of subject discipline**
   3. **Self-directed learning**
   4. **Communication skills**
   5. **Application to new situations**
   6. **Analysing an argument**
   7. **Invention**
   8. **Assessing quality**
We note that many teachers in higher education restrict their aims to Objectives 1 and 2, but even those who aspire to something more ambitious may ruin their students' opportunities by the examinations they set.

NOTES ON ACTIVITIES

Activity 1 I would expect a very heavy emphasis on memorizing information, relieved here and there by the exceptional teacher who took great trouble to enable pupils to understand what they were learning.

Activity 3 I would expect your report to show a stronger emphasis on the memorization of basic facts in disliked subjects and a greater emphasis on the explanation of ideas and on critical thinking in the subjects you enjoyed. In some cases, however, the source of your enjoyment would have been that the basic factual material was conveyed in a more exciting way.

3

Depth of study and vitality of learning

WHAT DO WE MEAN BY DEPTH OF STUDY?

... What happens when we concentrate on one thing 'in depth'? How does our world change? The answer varies from one person to another, but there are certain common experiences. Our sense of time is modified: we may look up from a book to find ... that two hours have passed without our noticing. We may become deeply immersed in what we are doing, not hearing the road-drill outside, and forgetting other things we had planned to do. *G. Squires* (12)

... But the language of depth is much more dramatic than this on some occasions. Mild-mannered academics will talk of 'really getting to grips with a problem ... wrestling with new difficulties ... finally getting on top of it ... getting one's teeth into it'. They will talk of 'hunting down references', 'penetrating to the heart of the matter' ... Students may complain of 'getting hopelessly lost ... stuck ... bogged down' on a course. (12)

In a detailed study of current practice in British universities and polytechnics a research team came up with some useful results: the two passages quoted above are from one of their reports. In many interviews with tutors and students they found that the concept of 'depth' of study or learning was repeatedly emphasized as an aim in its own right, not connected with 'breadth' of study.

Activity 1: Words 'Depth of study': what does this phrase mean to you from your own experience?

In these interviews, the phrase 'depth of study' was given various interpretations: a habit of getting to the core of the argument in a given article or discussion; a search for a personal meaning or relevance in the material; a certain receptiveness and alertness of mind, which is alive to unexpected evidence and alternative explanations and willing to question the assumptions underlying one's own and other people's thinking. It implies a recognition of the provisional nature of all knowledge, not only one's own but that of the 'authorities'; and a certain vitality or energy, an intensity of mental activity as one works on a subject, as Cardinal Newman so vividly described it in one of the passages quoted on pp. 6–7.

Activity 2: Words Give an example from your own experience to show what you mean by 'recognizing the provisional nature of all knowledge'.

FURTHER FINDINGS FROM RESEARCH

These qualities of mind are paralleled in the results of some illuminating research carried out among university students in Sweden, where the three main findings were as follows.

First, the investigators uncovered a clear distinction between a 'deep processing' of the material studied, or a 'deep approach' to it, and a 'surface processing' or 'surface approach'. An active deep approach is characterized by a search for the inner core of the argument, for personal relevance or meaning in the material, and a questioning, perhaps challenging, attitude to it. A surface approach tends to concentrate on memorizing unrelated facts or ideas.

The *deep* approach is vividly illustrated by the following excerpts from two students' reports on their work:

> . . . I was looking for the argument and whatever points were used to illustrate it. I could not avoid relating the article to other things I had read, past experience, and associations, etc. My feelings about

the issues raised made me hope he would present a more convincing argument than he did, so that I could formulate and adapt my ideas more closely, according to the reaction I felt to his argument. (14)

... Whilst reading the article, I took great care in trying to understand what the author was getting at, looking out for arguments, and facts which backed up the arguments I found myself continually relating the article to personal experience, and thus facilitated my understanding of it. (14)

The *surface* approach can be illustrated by the following student report:

... In reading the article I was looking out mainly for facts and examples. I read the article more carefully than I usually would, taking notes, knowing that I was to answer questions about it. I thought the questions would be about the facts in the article. This did influence the way I read; I tried to memorize names and figures quoted, etc. (14)

The close connection between the qualities of mind indicated by 'depth' of study or 'deep processing' and those of the higher order skills listed in chapter 2 is easy to see. Searching for the inner core of the argument in an article or chapter necessarily involves Objectives 6 (analysing an argument) and 8 (assessing quality). It means disentangling the various phases of the article and assessing their relative importance; deciding which parts are crucial, which are entirely irrelevant, which are relevant but of minor importance, and what is the backbone of the argument. Alertness of mind and receptiveness to unexpected evidence, and to alternative explanations of the data, are the qualities of mind that make Objective 7 (invention) attainable. They are the basis of inventiveness in solving unfamiliar problems or creating fresh schemes.

The 'surface' approach on the other hand is readily identified with Objective 1 (basic knowledge).

Activity 3: Stop, think and note When do you regularly use a 'deep' approach to your reading? When do you regularly use a 'surface' approach? How would you describe *your* experience of these two approaches?

The second main finding of the Swedish investigators was that students usually expect examination questions to test the array of facts that are acquired through a surface approach, but when they appreciate that the questions will test the kind of reasoning and the appreciation of argument which are acquired through a deep approach, they may try to switch to a deep approach. The third finding was that a surface approach tends to be associated with a sense in the student's mind that there is a vast syllabus to be assimilated if examinations are to be passed, and accordingly with a low level of interest and a high level of anxiety. As one African principal of a Bible College said, 'The syllabus is far too big, and this compels staff and students to depend on lectures and handouts: failure in the examination would be too disastrous.'

Activity 4: Stop, think and note Have you ever felt that you were faced with a vast syllabus to be assimilated if an examination was to be passed, so that you could not allow yourself to get deeply involved in any one area for fear of neglecting others, and were always anxious and nervous about your progress? Briefly describe the circumstances.

Emphasis on deep processing must not, however, be taken to imply a dismissal of surface processing; memorization of data and techniques is indispensable for certain purposes. Nor must it be taken to imply any uniformity in the way in which different people set about the deep or surface processing of material; individuals vary widely in their styles and techniques of study. We need to be very clear about the aims that in fact govern our practice, and what our priorities among them are to be. We also need to be versatile, and adapt our approach to the needs of our job.

Activity 5: Stop, think and note Select a subject you enjoyed in your last year at school or college. Do you think it should, or could, have been taught in a way that would have encouraged greater 'depth of study', in the sense given here? If so, how?

Activity 6: Stop, think and note Select a topic which you have yourself taught. Do you think you should, or could, have taught it in a way that would have encouraged greater depth of study? If so, how?

From these considerations it may be useful to formulate two subsidiary or parallel objectives for the student, relating to the higher order skills:

(a) To acquire a habit of *deep processing* of the material studied, i.e.

searching for the inner core of the argument in a given passage, and for its personal relevance or meaning.

(b) To acquire a habit of questioning and perhaps *challenging* the message conveyed; i.e. being aware of alternative interpretations and recognizing the provisional nature of the knowledge offered: in short, **questioning the message.**

SUMMARY

Reports from studies of British higher education show a great emphasis among both tutors and students on the importance of depth of study, and this concept is explored. Swedish researchers have provided evidence for an important distinction between 'deep' and 'surface' processing of the material studied by students. Hence two subsidiary objectives are formulated for students: deep processing of their academic sources, and questioning the message conveyed.

4

Existential understanding and practical judgement

BOOKS AND LIFE

... Let us consider how differently young and old are affected by the words of some classic author ... Passages which to a boy are but rhetorical commonplaces, neither better nor worse than a hundred others, at length come home to him, when long years have passed, and he has had experience of life, and pierce him, as if he had never before known them, with their sad earnestness and vivid exactness. *John Henry Newman* (6)

... Before this, words meant nothing to me; now they speak to me and I can make them speak. *A peasant, reported by Paulo Freire* (7)

... 'Practical' knowledge cannot be learned or taught prior to the activity itself but only acquired by practice in the activity. [In the sphere of public action] what has to be learned is not an abstract idea or set of tricks ... but a concrete coherent manner of living in all its intricateness. *Michael Oakeshott, quoted in* (15)

16

More than 2000 years ago the Greek historian Thucydides, writing about the Peloponnesian War of 431–404 BC which was so disastrous for Athens and its democracy, commented:

> These revolutions brought appalling sufferings on the Greek city states. In times of peace and prosperity nations and individuals alike follow higher standards because they are not forced into situations where they have to do what they do not want to do. But war is a savage teacher: it deprives men of the power of easily satisfying their daily needs and brings most people's characters down to the level of their actual circumstances. (*Adapted*)

What Thucydides wrote means a great deal more to people who have lived through a global world war or bitter civil war, or perhaps a long-running inter-tribal or inter-religious conflict, than it does to those who have only lived in times of peace. Our experience illuminates what we read in his book. Not only so: what we read may enable us to understand and interpret our experience the better. The influence of a savage war on our own standards of morality is illuminated by the historian's comment. Books and experience can illuminate one another; academic studies take on an existential meaning when their truth is deeply felt in a lived experience.

Activity 1: Stop, think and note Have you had the experience of re-reading something in adult life which seemed trivial when you read it while you were at school but now seems to be saying something important? If so, write a short account of it.

If we turn to the Bible we can find further examples of this mutual illumination of books and events. In Amos, for instance, we find denunciations of Israel in the 8th century BC:

> Thus says the Lord . . .
> because they sell the righteous for silver,
> and the needy for a pair of shoes —
> they that trample the head of the poor into the dust of the
> earth . . .
> Behold, I will press you down in your place,
> as a cart full of sheaves presses down.
> Flight shall perish from the swift,
> and the strong shall not retain his strength,
> nor shall the mighty save his life. (Amos 2.6–7, 13–14)

The people of Judah saw Amos's judgement on the Northern Kingdom proved true when that Kingdom collapsed. And nearly 200 years later, in 587 BC, when Jerusalem itself was destroyed and many of Judah's people were sent into exile in Babylon, they saw that his words applied to them also. It was only then that they grasped the full meaning of his warnings.

Unfortunately, however, the learning given in colleges and universities is too often bookish and nothing else. A common criticism of tertiary education is that students acquire a lot of 'book-learning', but little skill in using this learning in everyday life. Prominent industrialists, for example, have declared that many graduates fail to match up to the demands of industrial jobs. Too often they are unable to apply their hard-won knowledge to the complex economic/manufacturing/political problems of the industrial world, and find it hard to make decisions in real situations.

Activity 2: Stop, think and note Have you had the experience of finding yourself unsure of what action to take over a problem which you have studied in books and lectures at college? If so, describe it briefly.

And indeed Christian workers in the field sometimes claim that the study of academic theology not only divorces one's thinking from the problems of the communities one is supposed to serve, but channels one's intellectual effort towards books and speculation.

Book-learning has always tended to diverge from the demands and experience of daily life; but this tendency has been enormously increased during the twentieth century by the extraordinary explosion of knowledge. As a result the universities and colleges primarily involved with the creation and dissemination of this knowledge have given an ever-increasing emphasis to its extension and refinement. Most of the problems which the academic world deals with are generated and solved within the subject disciplines themselves. The careers of teachers in tertiary education today depend more and more on their achievement in research, and on the reputation they gain among senior fellow workers in other institutions and other countries. Thus teachers have become more and more preoccupied with research, and students have become more and more intimidated by the volume of knowledge crowding into their syllabuses.

We discuss the various responses to these developments in the next three sections.

TACIT KNOWLEDGE

In the first place, educationists now recognize that much learning takes place which does not give one explicit knowledge that can be explained in words to another person. Instead it produces a kind of knowledge which is rarely put into words, the 'tacit' knowledge, which everybody has, of people and situations and trains of events, and of the way things function and materials behave. This is not gained from theoretical instruction or book study. We learn it through our interaction with other people and with the multitude of objects and events we encounter in daily living. Many experienced and wise people reach decisions for action, not by explicit analysis but through intuitive insight, through the development of a practical judgement. And this judgement often proves to be right. Tacit knowledge is the basis of much professional expertise. A midwife, for example, depends on a gradually growing knowledge of many individual mothers from many different backgrounds, in many situations. A politician develops an 'instinct' for judging a political climate, assessing the temper of a constituency, or sensing the mood of a parliament. And a Church leader too learns to exercise a similar intuitive 'practical judgement'.

Activity 3: Stop, think and note Give an example of a human situation in which you consider that you usually make the right decision without putting it into words. Describe, in as much detail as you can, just how you think it out.

Traditional education and training in many different cultures was based on this pattern. For example, the African Principal of a Bible College who had spent three years studying at Harvard University and other colleges in the USA told how, on taking up his post as Principal, he was obliged to put his academic learning aside and use the understanding and know-how he had acquired as he grew up in an extended family within his tribe. This understanding was rarely put into words, but it was a sure guide to action. Scripture similarly shows that the 'wisdom' of good rulers was seen as a practical judgement of men and affairs. In Ecclesiasticus, for example, we find:

... On the other hand he who devotes himself
to the study of the law of the Most High
will seek out the wisdom of the ancients,
and will be concerned with prophecies;
he will preserve the discourse of notable men
and penetrate the subtleties of parables;
he will seek out the hidden meanings of proverbs
and be at home with the obscurities of parables.
He will serve among great men

and appear before rulers;
he will travel through the lands of foreign nations,
for he tests the good and the evil among men.

In addition, as this passage continues, the wise ruler will 'seek the Lord':

... He will set his heart to rise early
to seek the Lord who made him,
and he will make supplication before the Most High;
he will open his mouth in prayer
and make supplication for his sins. (Ecclus. 39.1–5)

Moreover the Bible shows very clearly that to know God is to practise righteousness and do justice, as Jeremiah declares:

... Did not your father eat and drink
and do justice and righteousness?
Then it was well with him.
He judged the cause of the poor and needy;
then it was well.
It not this to know me?
says the Lord. (Jer. 22. 15–16)

And again:

... let him who glories glory in this, that he understands and knows me, that I am the Lord who practise steadfast love, justice, and righteousness in the earth; for in these things I delight, says the Lord. (Jer. 9. 24)

So we have a picture of the wise ruler as one who learns from others older and wiser than himself, in whatever country, and faithfully serves God who practises 'steadfast love, justice and righteousness'.

USING ACADEMIC KNOWLEDGE IN PRACTICAL ENTERPRISES

In the second place, educationists now recognize that the long-standing assumption, that one must *first acquire* mastery of certain academic learning and *subsequently apply* it to the practical world, is no more than a myth. This assumption is implied by our Objective 4 (application in new situations); but careful observation of the realities of the practical world points to something rather different.

If, for example, we look at the way we deal with the problems and predicaments of ordinary life, we see something like the following. At first we are aware of a difficulty or deficiency—say, the lack of facilities for holding a large fundraising event. We think all round it, carefully distinguishing what is essential from what is not. That is, we define as precisely as we can what the problem or task is.

Secondly, we assemble all available information relating to the problem—all the aspects to be considered and all possible ways of overcoming it.

Third, we analyse all this information, trying out some ideas in detail, grappling with any snags, eliminating what is not practical or strictly relevant.

Eventually an idea for practical action emerges, which then has to be shaped for realization. For some sorts of problem the next stage might be a trial run, followed by evaluation and final adjustment, before the scheme is put into practice. Lastly comes the assessment of its effectiveness.

Activity 4: Stop, think and note Think back to any scheme or plan you have had to work out—visiting a relative or friend who lives at a distance, moving house, buying a car. Analyse your procedure and check how far the account given in the above section matches up to what you actually did.

Detailed observations of practitioners at work in a number of professions—doctors, architects, managers—also show that in these processes there is an intimate, subtle interweaving of *ideas*, whether derived from books or colleagues or earlier experience, with the detailed queries provoked by the *actual situation* that the practitioner is tackling.

Activity 5: Stop, think and note Think back to how you tackled a specific task in your ministry or profession. What stages of trial and error did you go through? Where did you get the various ideas that you tried out as you went along?

EDUCATION FOR CAPABILITY

Thirdly, alongside these reinterpretations of how people become skilled in the arts of living and working, institutions of tertiary education are being specifically challenged to adapt their practice more closely to the real future needs of their graduates. The purposes that predominate in these institutions, especially universities, largely match our Objectives 1–8, but the advocates of this new approach demand greater emphasis on education for 'capability for everyday living'. This implies reasonable competence in one's job and one's recreations, and also a capacity to cope with the problems, pressures and complexities of daily living—in short, skill in managing one's life. Another element is the capacity to invent, create, and construct schemes and objects—something very close to our Objective 7. And a fourth element is a capacity for getting on with other people, whether in work or in everyday social life, implying a developed sense of mutual dependence and support.

Activity 6: Words Give several examples from your own experience of the ways in which young people are trained for 'capability' in post-secondary education.

Parallel to this line of thought there have been moves in many universities and colleges to relate the bookish studies more closely to students' first-hand experience of the real world, and enable them to develop some degree of practical judgement in dealing with its daily contingencies. Many colleges now organize field studies, in which students can relate their book-work to direct experience. For example, a student of botany spends a day making a systematic study of a small area of ground; a student of geography spends a week examining the form and development of a certain district; a student of engineering spends a year working in an industrial firm, and a theological student is given a placement where he will participate in Christian witness and Church activity.

Activity 7: Stop, think and note Give two or three examples of field work you have carried out as part of an academic course. What aspects of *academic* work did they help you to understand? What part if any did you think was a waste of time? What do you consider were the real benefits of the experience?

For the in-service training of industrial managers many firms find it profitable to work together in a joint scheme of development. Each of five or six firms specifies a particular management problem which it faces, and designates a senior staff member to act as Consultant Fellow to one of the other firms for (say) six months, to explore that problem. The visiting Fellows are naturally ignorant of the way their host firms function and need to ask many questions about the firm and its problem. They meet as a group each week to debate the problems, and their findings, and also have a working contact with a university or polytechnic Business School. Eventually they produce reports diagnosing the problems and offering tentative solutions.

In carrying out these jobs the Fellows find several things happening. The arguments in the weekly group meetings generate intense involvement in the business of analysing the problems and producing practical solutions. They find it less and less possible to hide their ignorance or mistaken opinions behind excuses or bluff. Their judgement of what is practicable in a given concrete situation becomes much clearer and firmer; and the firms begin to catch the habit of asking searching questions on the way they work, and of reflecting on that experience. This system, known as 'Action Learning', offers practical possibilities for theological students engaged in longer field projects.

In these activities students, whether undergraduates or trainee managers, gain in two rather different ways. First, they acquire a lot of new tacit knowledge of their fellows, and of employers and workplaces, and have a chance to develop their 'practical judgement of people and situations'. They also see that the knowledge they acquire from books is in fact the basis of many activities and processes in the workplace; and their dry bookish knowledge comes alive when its implications and applications are seen in practice. The interweaving of academic study with first-hand experience of the 'real world' is at the same time a marrying of academically-derived ideas with the tacit unverbalized knowledge of direct experience. We could say that the book-learning illuminates the experience and the experience the book-learning. The book-learning gains an existential meaning from being seen in the context of a lived reality.

Activity 8: Words Explain in a few sentences what the word 'existential' means to you.

All these considerations apply with special force to a student of the Christian faith, with its biblical and theological spheres of learning. Few theological students are primarily concerned with the 'academic' study of theology, divorced from its bearing on the realities of daily living. Most are searching for a deeper understanding of the faith, and of the interrelationship of their academic studies with the problems encountered in the everyday world. The interweaving of theoretical principles and 'real world' experiences is vividly attested by those who organize TEE courses in Latin America. Ross Kinsler, for instance, comments that 'by placing the academic as well as the practical aspects of training in the normal context of life and ministry, it may be possible to integrate them more effectively in relation to real human problems', when the providers of courses 'are sitting down with local leaders and beginning to reflect on the real and felt needs of [their] people and to discuss how to meet those needs in the light of the Gospel' (1),(2). A project in South India illustrates one approach. A theological seminary there has developed a model farm where students spend part of their time, and which serves as a centre for community work in the area, among untouchables and the prosperous as well. There is no direct evangelism, but the gospel is demonstrated in action, and students engage in searching discussions on the nature of sin, the role of the Church in a context of social conflict, etc. In this way, abstract theological concepts acquire an existential significance for the students, over and above their 'academic' meaning. Thus we see that an intimate interaction can be established between *thinking* about God's action in the world and *living out* His will in the community in which one actually lives and works—between *action* in a social context and *reflection* on the meaning and interpretation of that experience. There are, however, certain areas of these studies which are not touched by this kind of engagement, where the problem of enabling students to take their book learning into their mental furniture has to be approached in other ways.

IN WHAT SENSE THE 'REAL WORLD'?

References to the 'real world', to 'real human problems', can be understood in two different ways.

First, they may relate to the wide range of problems we encounter in our personal lives—in our jobs, our marriages, our families, where we feel them most immediately and acutely; and also in the obscure questioning and deeper search for a meaning in life, which are an inescapable element of human existence. For potential Church leaders 'capability for coping with the problems of life' is not to be interpreted in a narrow sense; the universal questions need also to be taken into account. What sort of people are we in reality? What does it mean to be 'authentic' persons, our real selves rather than merely followers of fashion or slaves to custom? What does it mean to treat others as real authentic persons? In our context one of the aims will be to help students to reflect on such questions and gain some insight into the culture-bound nature of our most certain knowledge; in short, to get an existential understanding of those awkward questions about the meaning of life.

For a college engaged in training Church leaders, whether clergy or lay, these questions must pass into the specific areas of prayer and worship, and into that process of Christian development we have described (p. 3) as 'learning to develop a depth of commitment, a conviction of the reality of God's love, and a continuing growth towards some profound trust in Jesus'; or in St Paul's succinct phrase 'putting on Christ'.

In the second place such phrases as the 'real world' may equally refer to the problems we encounter as members of a community, where the community as a whole is faced with difficult, even desperate, situations, such as drought and famine in parts of Africa, multiple deprivation in India, or oppression in a police state in Latin America. These problems of the economic or political structure of a society immediately raise questions about the Church's proper sphere of influence, especially for institutions run by the Church. There has been a longstanding division of opinion between those who regard the province of the Church as properly restricted to the maintenance of congregational worship and the pastoral care of individuals and families, and those who believe that over and above these duties the Church must also concern itself with the structural features of society which govern people's living conditions. This latter position raises questions about the precise nature of 'the Church', and about the practical character of the involvement of the clergy with the economic/political/structural aspects of everyday life. Some ministers and pastors tend to identify themselves too exclusively with the communities in which they are working and serving. Ministers and lay leaders in a deprived community are apt to slide into a one-sided political commitment; and so too are those working mainly among the affluent and politically powerful. However, as Gutiérrez indicates (56), a more comprehensive analysis of the structural aspects of society is likely to show that ministry at either level is incomplete without adequate attention to the other. Our concern here is with the existential understanding of academic studies and the development of a practical judgement of people and human situations.

Activity 9: Stop, think and note Describe briefly any unit of study about the Christian faith which you have *either* studied *or* taught in a context of the real problems of a community, a family or individual. To what extent did you feel it was necessary for you to identify yourself with a political grouping? or to *avoid* identifying yourself with a political grouping? Explain your reasons.

These considerations point to a further objective to add to our list:

Objective 9. To acquire an existential understanding of academic subject matter and develop a practical judgement of people and situations: in short, **existential understanding and practical judgement.**

SUMMARY

The chapter is concerned with the interrelationships between the knowledge gained from books and first-hand experience. The tendency for the two to part company has been accentuated by the explosion of knowledge that has taken place in the twentieth century. There have been three types of response to this situation. First, educationists have emphasized that much of the knowledge that human beings acquire, particularly knowledge of people and situations, is never put into words: it remains 'tacit', unverbalized. Second, observation has shown that academic knowledge, as normally acquired through formal instruction, rarely gets applied to practical situations: the process of interplay is both subtler and more intimate. Third, there has been a growing demand in various parts of the world for tertiary education to train students not so much for a career in academic research or teaching as for 'capability' in the affairs of the 'real world'. A final section explores the different senses of the phrase 'the real world', namely the private world of families and feelings and the public world of economic, social and political activity.

NOTES ON ACTIVITIES

Activity 4 My guess is that you would report a long period of trial and error and that the ideas and methods you eventually established as a routine came from a variety of sources: friends' advice, casual conversation, academic tutorials and occasionally books.

Activity 7 I would expect you to report that you had only the vaguest idea of what academic material your field work was supposed to illuminate, but that you gained enormously in experience of the world of work and in practical judgement of people and affairs.

5

Group discussion and collaboration

SOME REMARKS ON WORKING IN GROUPS

... A student's colleagues often represent the least recognized, least used and possibly the most important of all the resources available to him. *N. Mackenzie and others* (25)

... Our experience with really effective groups has been so limited that we do not have clear standards of what could be. *D. McGregor* (26)

The following comments (quoted in G. Collier (27)) are all from students working in small groups of five or six members.

... This group ... has stimulated all of us intellectually. So many more ideas and concepts are brought out when discussing in an informal situation than being alone to think or in a large group ... Someone was always there to refute or elaborate on someone else's ideas in a frank manner.

... This entire course has triggered in me a want and motivation for research, references and critical thinking, which is developing for the first time.

... One of the good things about this method is that it's not just one person seeking out information and then imparting it to the whole lecture group, but you have four or five different people who are going out and seeking information along their own track and then coming back to the group and then explaining round the group and discussing from four or five different points of view.

... Much of the class time was spent in small-group discussion to which the members of the group developed loyalty (this was expressed by members of our syndicate) and felt responsibility to do their part and even to explore further books and relate class work to work previously taken. As a result an independent attitude was developed by many of the students who went out and purchased some of the suggested books or read parts of them in the library, going beyond the minimum standards set by the professor and the group.

DISCUSSION WORK IN TERTIARY EDUCATION

Much attention has been given to the use of discussion techniques in post-school education, and it is now widely accepted that most students learn about their subjects with greater clarity and richness through interaction with their peers. A leading twentieth-century psychologist, Jean Piaget, has emphasized the significance of interaction within peer groups. The hammering out of ideas and views in groups is vital for training people to analyse their thinking and appreciate the importance of precise definitions and clear concepts. The first two students' comments quoted above illustrate the intellectual rewards gained from working in groups. The use of discussion also helps to generate habits and skills of co-operation, and a sense of commitment, in the carrying out of complex tasks which call for analysis and planning. The third and fourth of the students' comments convey something of the impact of small-group work in a broader context.

COLLABORATIVE WORKING WORLDWIDE

The expansion of technical developments in industrialized countries has given rise to radical changes in the way professional people work, including ordained clergy and lay leaders. These are all likely to be employed throughout their professional careers in teams or groups, perhaps in medical teams, or in local government, or in inter-disciplinary groups assembled to tackle (for example) the problem of clean water-supply in a developing country.

Activity 1: Stop, think and note Report briefly an experience in which you worked with a small group of colleagues—not more than six in number—on a task of some kind, whether academic or otherwise. What benefits were gained? What satisfaction did you get? What problems arose? What kinds of training do you think would be advisable for a small team of this sort to be most effective?

Activity 2: Words 'Inter-disciplinary teams': explain the meaning of the phrase, using a different example from that used in the text.

People today are also much more concerned about the power exercised by experts and by large business corporations and even government agencies. Some countries have a long tradition of lay control over professional experts. Educational institutions and local

government agencies have customarily been governed by lay committees, whether elected or appointed. The ultimate decision in many
courts of law rests with a jury of lay people rather than judges or
advocates. There is a growing demand for more widely-based participation by the public in decisions affecting them, for example in urban
development or the siting of new roads. In many countries public
opinion soon makes its weight felt through the media.

Activity 3: Stop, think and note Outline some experience of your
own *either* as a leader *or* as a follower, in which followers were
encouraged to participate with the leader in planning some action
or reaching some decision. How real was the involvement of the
followers? What limits were set beyond which they could not go?
How were these limits maintained?

Activity 4: Stop, think and note What do you understand by the
phrase 'lay control over professional experts'? Have you any
experience of such a structure in your own country? If so, describe
it briefly. If not, search out an example from your library.

These generalizations, however, do not apply everywhere. All industrialized societies have areas of poverty and deprivation, where people
lack the knowledge, skills, and confidence, to make the social system
in which they live serve their own needs. They are not necessarily
starving to death or dying of treatable diseases, but they perceive
themselves as powerless and disregarded, and are unable to gain for
themselves a stable and respected status, whether economic or political.

In South and Central America, for example, many communities
perceive themselves as powerless and disregarded in this way, and
there has been a phenomenal growth among them of what have come
to be more widely known as 'base' or 'basic' Christian communities.
These are small groups who meet for Bible study and prayer, share
common concerns, and work together to build a more human society.
These groups are in desperate need of trained leaders, far beyond the
number of clergy that the mother Churches could supply. Training
courses for local lay leaders therefore need to include not only biblical
and theological studies and pastoral training, but also systematic
opportunities for learning the skills of team work and how to teach
those skills to others.

There can however be problems. When a community or organization first begins to feel its power, it may become over-confident or
aggressive. It may build up expectations which are self-defeating
because they involve too sharp or sudden a break with the past; that

is, too sharp to be accepted as right or fair by the natural leaders of opinion. On the other hand, the leaders of worker/peasant groups may be subtly assimilated into existing power groups, and in effect act as their agents. In many areas the main problem may be that of finding potential Christian leaders within the deprived community. Where the affluent have taken up entrenched positions and the poor are desperate, political and personal skills of a very high order are needed in leaders on both sides, if the mobilizing of community opinion is not to result in violent conflict. In short, the training of Church leaders in team work and community development is immensely important.

Activity 5: Words 'Basic Christian communities': do you know of any small Christian groups or congregations trying to sustain themselves, perhaps isolated from other congregations or from outside assistance? Write 300 words on what you think are or could be their main problems.

IMPLICATIONS FOR TERTIARY EDUCATION

At whatever social level clergy or lay Church leaders are operating, they obviously need a highly developed capacity for working closely with other people. This may be with fellow members of their own profession or with members of other professions, with highly educated or minimally educated people, with the old or the young, with members of a closely-related culture or of one that is very different. They need a clear understanding of different styles of authority, different ways of building up relationships, different procedures for reaching decisions, different forms of interaction between cultures. The idea of 'skills' in this context may be too restrictive, a better description might be 'competencies'.

At this point we must consider a specifically Christian aspect of group collaboration for which Bible writers used the Greek work *koinonia*, meaning something like 'fellowship' or 'communion' or 'sharing'. This points to a community in which the barriers of racial hatred, and of conflict, mistrust and oppression between social classes, different cultures, rich and poor, masters and slaves, are broken down, dissolved away. In putting on Christ, St Paul wrote, 'there is neither Jew nor Greek, there is neither slave nor free, there is neither male nor female; for you are all one in Christ Jesus' (Gal.3. 28). 'So if there is any encouragement in Christ, any incentive of love, any participation in the spirit, any affection and sympathy, complete my joy by being of the same mind, having the same love' (Phil. 2.1). Such an ideal goes far beyond skill or competence in collaborating effectively with other people, and we must admit that most Christians still have much to learn about how to work in harmony with others.

However, in emphasizing the power and harmonious relationships of 'koinonia' we also need to recognize that a group may become *too* absorbed in its own togetherness. Over-cohesive and self-absorbed groups are found particularly in religious bodies, in sports teams, and in the armed forces. A glaring example was that of the American President John Kennedy and his team of outstandingly able advisers, who prepared the disastrous 'invasion' at the Bay of Pigs in Cuba. The only explanation seems to be that they developed too intense a feeling of in-group identity, which blinded them to wider considerations.

Here, then, is an aim which few universities or colleges build into their curricula, and this has been the subject of frequent criticism by employers. It is obviously too important to omit from our list, and so becomes:

Objective 10: To acquire the skills or competencies of effective collaboration with other people: in short, **team work skills.**

SUMMARY

In recent years discussion work in tertiary education has considerably increased, prompted partly by the extension of collaborative work in many occupations regarded in the past as involving largely one-to-one practitioner/client relationships. There has also been a spread of collaboration between people in economic and political situations of low status, in order to get their voices heard and their needs met. Hence the implication that tertiary education should be providing some training in the skills of collaboration: in short, **team work skills.**

NOTE ON ACTIVITIES

Activity 2 'Inter-disciplinary teams': the phrase means teams of workers drawn from several academic disciplines: for example, a team to produce recommendations for overcoming atmospheric pollution would need to include a chemist with skill in the measurement of the pollution, a geologist with skills in tracing the mineral sources of the materials causing pollution, heating engineers with knowledge of the various ways in which fuel can be burned to give heat, an economist who can calculate the overall economic impact of prevention methods, a sociologist and a geographer to look at the human implications of any proposed changes. Similar multi-disciplinary teams could be organized to establish, for example, fish farming or cotton growing.

6
Culture clashes and the ethical dimension

A CASE STUDY FROM AFRICA

Example 1

Let us imagine a village called, say, Tandara. If Tandara is made up of segments of two or three local clans [or groups of families], they see it as a unit with two or three sub-divisions. And the important thing is this: the way in which the people see their village's structure will affect the ways in which they behave . . . If Tandara is made up of two or three parts, then on some occasions they will act as separate units and on some occasions, when all the separate units are involved, they will act as one village, as a unity . . .

I remember that, after we baptized the Chokosi village of Famisa, I told the people they should appoint presbyters. I read out the characteristics recommended for Church leaders in 1 Timothy 3, and asked the villagers to select out of their number those who they felt could serve well. Then, I said, we would vote. I asked for nominations. The chief turned to the elder of his own local clan and said 'Should we appoint Sanda to stand for us?' The elder agreed. He then turned to the head of another local clan: 'Ananji, who will stand for the Fombolo people?'

I stopped him. 'You don't seem to understand', I said, 'You are to appoint two men for the first 20 communicants and one man for every other

20 communicants. The clans and houses don't matter. There are 40 male communicants in this congregation. You get three presbyters. Anyone can be nominated; and everyone will vote, and those who get the most votes will serve for a trial year.'

The chief did not understand. Nor did he try very hard. He continued to proceed as before. One man was chosen by each section of the village and no others were nominated. There was no vote. Unbelieving, I said to the people, 'Do you all agree with those who have been chosen?' They looked at me, wondering why I was so dull.

And I was dull. I just didn't see Famisa in the way they did. I still thought it was a collection of individuals. I didn't realize it was a village with three parts. I didn't know what these parts were, local clans, nor how they were related to each other as a village. *The village* had been baptized, not just the individual people. And the village, as a congregation of the Church, would be led as the village had always been led, by representatives of each of its three local clans. That was the only way in which an effective local Church council could be formed in Famisa. To try to break down these units into a collection of individuals, and then vote, would have been to break up the customary social structure of Famisa into an unworkable confusion. The people were very sensible when they refused to listen to me. (A. C. Krass, *Go . . . and make disciples* TEF Study Guide 9 (29))

ENCOUNTERS BETWEEN CULTURES

A characteristic feature of late twentieth-century society is the increasingly close meeting and interchange of people of different cultures, different ways of life, different outlooks and values. We use the word 'culture' here in the anthropological sense, as *the web or fabric of customs, meanings, relationships and values which characterize any given society or community.* Paulo Freire speaks of a 'people's view of the world: a view which explicitly and implicitly contains their concerns, their doubts, their way of seeing their leaders, their perceptions of themselves and of the oppressors, their religious beliefs . . ., their fatalism, their rebellious reactions. None of these elements can be seen separately, for in interaction all of them compose a totality' (7). Dr Krass's experience at Famisa illustrates the effect of an encounter between people of widely different cultures, in the shape of mutual incomprehension and failure of communication between the missionary and the African chief.

Activity 1: Words In about 300 words outline the main features of the *culture* of any small group you have belonged to, whether in adult life or during your school days.

In the past there was far less mass movement of people about the world; most individuals remained throughout their lives within relatively self-contained cultures. In the twentieth century huge numbers of refugees have moved to other countries—in Europe, America, Africa, India, China. Very many holiday-makers visit other countries for short spells, and vast numbers of ordinary citizens are made aware by radio and television of the contrasts and contradictions between different cultures in the world at large, and between sub-cultures within their own society.

A SPECIFIC CULTURE CLASH

To clarify and sharpen the argument we now look at a specific episode of culture clash, as described in a report on the commissioning of an American chemical plant in Europe (30). The American firm ran into problems during its regular planning meetings with representatives of the European firm. The Americans assumed that any staff member with expertise in a particular aspect should make his own specialist contribution. But their European clients did not share this view. They expected that their senior representatives would present their own personal views as forcefully as they could, wearing down the opposition until—if possible—a single view prevailed. The Americans saw the situation as one where different individuals with different kinds of expertise had complementary parts to play in the handling of a specific problem; they set a high value on a spirit of co-operation and the working out of a common view to which all members would contribute and be loyal. The Europeans saw the situation as one in which senior members competed for dominance; they set a high value on the forceful and persistent arguing of contrasting views, with junior members keeping in the background. In short, the two sides had contrasting *perceptions* of the situation, and contrasting sets of values. This word 'values' needs a little explanation. As used here it refers to *those objects, or conditions of living, or ways of behaving, on which people set a value or which they regard as important*. This means not simply their explicit intentions, at a conscious level, but the underlying forces, *the driving purposes or aspirations of their lives*. In this case each side tended to suspect the motives and distrust the competence of the other, with obvious consequences in the shape of misunderstanding and possible conflict.

Similar processes were at work in the missionary's encounter in the village of Famisa. Dr Krass saw the village as composed of separate individuals conscious of their own identity and freedom of action. But the people of Famisa themselves saw their community as made up of three groups of families, or clans, each functioning in most matters as a coherent group in which all members shared the clan identity. Dr Krass set a high value on individual decision-making, on each person's right to make individual choices, and on a sharing only at the level of a voting procedure. The Famisa people set a high value on conforming to the customs of the tribe, leaving most decision-making to the chiefs or elders, and in any big venture, like joining the Christian faith, on acting as a clan or community under their leadership. We find similar features in many other cultures and sub-cultures.

Activity 2: Stop, think and note Outline briefly a minor dispute in which you were involved in some organization or community. State what you think were (a) the participants' opposed perceptions of the situation, and (b) the participants' different values or priorities among their values.

A BIBLICAL CASE

We find another example in the semi-political religious groups that were active in Judea in the time of Jesus. The Sadducees were wealthy members of old families, from whom the high priests and elders were recruited. In religion they were ultra-conservative, but in life-style they leaned towards Greek customs. Their political ideal was a Jewish national state centred on the Temple.

The Pharisees were a highly respected and highly educated group who upheld the full authority of both the written Law of the Scriptures and the unwritten Law of established tradition. Their life was not centred on the Temple, but on the many local synagogues where the main teaching of the Law and interpretation of the Scriptures took place.The ideal of the Pharisees was to lead a blameless life in obedience to the Scriptures, with the reward of eternal life after bodily death.

Although the dividing lines between these groups were not as sharp as we have drawn them, the contrast between the two sub-cultures is clear enough. The Sadducees saw themselves as guardians of the Temple tradition. They had no belief in an after-life, and so centred their hopes on a politically independent Jewish state with the Temple at its heart. They gave highest priority to maintenance of the Temple in all its functions, and for this were willing to collaborate in some degree wth their Roman rulers.

The Pharisees on the other hand saw themselves as guardians of the Law. They gave highest priority to study of the Law and faithful obedience to it. Believing in the resurrection of the dead, they hoped for salvation not in a Jewish state but in eternal life.

Both groups, however, regarded the Romans as alien rulers and the Jewish people as chosen by God to maintain His worship and to obey His Law. And *both* attached a very high value to upholding those traditions.

A CULTURE CLASH WITHIN THE CHURCH

As these examples show, the unvoiced assumptions which people bring to situations of culture clash are not easy to identify, let alone to describe fully in words. Often it is difficult to discern precisely what the underlying forces are in a culture clash. The following example, from Bernard Shaw's play *Saint Joan* (32), shows how complex that task may be, and what profound differences of perceptions and values may be at work.

Example 2

Joan of Arc, a French peasant girl born in 1412, was inspired to lead the French forces to drive out the English, who at that time ruled part of France. She was captured and handed over to the English commander, who judged it advisable to pass her over to the ecclesiastical authorities, to be tried as a witch and a heretic who refused to accept the Church's ruling. In the following passage from Shaw's play it is 1431, and Joan is standing before the Church's court of justice at Rouen. The two judges are Bishop Cauchon and the Inquisitor (an ecclesiastical officer). D'Estivet is the prosecutor who formulates the case against Joan, and Ladvenu is a young Dominican monk sympathetic to her. The Assessors are Church officials responsible for co-ordinating the evidence and fanatically hostile to Joan. One of them, Canon de Courcelles, is intent on bringing forward any scrap of evidence, however dubious, to discredit her.

Cauchon [Bishop of the diocese]: Come! we are wasting time on trifles. Joan: I am going to put a most solemn question to you. Take care how you answer; for your life and salvation are at stake on it. Will you for all you have said and done, be it good or bad, accept the judgement of God's Church on earth? More especially as to the acts and words that are imputed to you in this trial by the Promoter (*the prosecutor, Canon d'Estivet*] here, will you submit your case to the inspired interpretation of the Church Militant?
Joan: I am a faithful child of the Church. I will obey the Church—
Cauchon (hopefully leaning forward): You will?
Joan: —provided it does not command anything impossible.
Cauchon sinks back in his chair with a heavy sigh. The Inquisitor [a Dominican monk investigating heresy] purses his lips and frowns. Ladvenu [a young Dominican] shakes his head pitifully.
D'Estivet: She imputes to the Church the error and folly of commanding the impossible.

Joan: If you command me to declare that all that I have done and said, and all the revelations and visions I have had, were not from God, then that is impossible: I will not declare it for anything in the world. What God made me do I will never go back on; and what he has commanded or shall command I will not fail to do in spite of any man alive. That is what I mean by impossible. And in case the Church should bid me do anything contrary to the command I have from God, I will not consent to it, no matter what it may be.

The Assessors (shocked and indignant): Oh! The Church contrary to God! What do you say now? Flat heresy. This is beyond everything, etc., etc.

D'Estivet (throwing down his brief): My Lord: do you need anything more than this?

Cauchon: Woman: you have said enough to burn ten heretics. Will you not be warned? Will you not understand?

The Inquisitor: If the Church Militant tells you that your revelations and visions are sent by the devil to tempt you to your damnation, will you not believe that the Church is wiser than you?

Joan: I believe that God is wiser than I; and it is his commands that I will do. All the things that you call my crimes have come to me by the command of God: I say that I have done them by the order of God: it is impossible for me to say anything else. If any Churchman says the contrary I shall not mind him: I shall mind God alone, whose command I always follow.

Ladvenu (pleading with her urgently): You do not know what you are saying, child. Do you want to kill yourself? Listen. Do you not believe that you are subject to the Church of God on earth?

Joan: Yes. When have I ever denied it?

Ladvenu: Good. That means, does it not, that you are subject to our Lord the Pope, to the cardinals, the archbishops, and the bishops for whom his lordship stands here today?

Joan: God must be served first.

D'Estivet: Then your voices command you not to submit yourself to the Church Militant?

Joan: My voices do not tell me to disobey the Church; but God must be served first.

Cauchon: And you, and not the Church, are to be the judge?

Joan: What other judgement can I judge by but my own?

The Assessors (scandalized): Oh! (*They cannot find words.*)

Cauchon: Out of your own mouth you have condemned yourself. We have striven for your salvation to the verge of sinning ourselves: we have opened the door to you again and again; and you have shut it in our faces and in the face of God. Dare you pretend, after what you have said, that you are in a state of grace?

Joan: If I am not, may God bring me to it: if I am, may God keep me in it!

Ladvenu: That is a very good reply, my lord.

Courcelles [a young priest]: Were you in a state of grace when you stole the Bishop's horse?

Cauchon (rising in a fury): Oh, devil take the Bishop's horse and you too! We are here to try a case of heresy; and no sooner do we come to the root of the matter than we are thrown back by idiots who understand nothing but horses. (*Trembling with rage, he forces himself to sit down.*)

The Inquisitor: Gentlemen, gentlemen: in clinging to these small issues you are The Maid's best advocates! I am not surprised that his lordship has lost patience with you. What does the Promoter say? Does he press these trumpery matters?

D'Estivet: I am bound by my office to press everything; but when the woman confesses a heresy that must bring upon her the doom of excommunication, of what consequence is it that she has been guilty also of offences which expose her to minor penances? I share the impatience of his lordship as to these minor charges. Only, with great respect, I must emphasize the gravity of two very horrible and blasphemous crimes which she does not deny. First, she has intercourse with evil spirits, and is therefore a sorceress. Second, she wears men's clothes, which is indecent, unnatural, and abominable; and in spite of our most earnest remonstrances and entreaties, she will not change them even to receive the sacrament.

Joan: Is the blessed St Catherine an evil spirit? Is St Margaret? Is Michael the Archangel?

Courcelles: How do you know that the spirit which appears to you is an archangel? Does he not appear to you as a naked man?

Joan: Do you think God cannot afford clothes for him?

(The Assessors cannot help smiling, especially as the joke is against Courcelles.)

Ladvenu: Well answered, Joan.

Inquisitor: It is, in effect, well answered. But no evil spirit would be so simple as to appear in a guise that would scandalize her when he meant her to take him for a messenger from the Most High. Joan: the Church instructs you that these apparitions are demons seeking your soul's perdition. Do you accept the instruction of the Church?

Joan: I accept the messenger of God. How could any faithful believer in the Church refuse him?

Cauchon: Wretched woman: again I ask you, do you know what you are saying?

Inquisitor: You wrestle in vain with the devil for her soul, my lord: she will not be saved. Now as to this matter of the man's dress. For the last time, will you put off that impudent attire, and dress as becomes your sex?

Joan: I will not.

D'Estivet (pouncing): The sin of disobedience, my lord.

Joan (distressed): But my voices tell me I must dress as a soldier.

Ladvenu: Joan, Joan: does not that prove to you that the voices are the voices of evil spirits? Can you suggest to us one good reason why an angel of God should give you such shameless advice?

Joan: Why, yes: what can be plainer commonsense? I was a soldier living among soldiers. I am a prisoner guarded by soldiers. If I were to dress as a woman they would think of me as a woman; and then what would become of me? If I dress as a soldier they think of me as a soldier, and I can live with them as I do at home with my brothers.

A close study of this scene—leaving aside the political calculations and the cruder prejudices of the participants—reveals that Cauchon and his ecclesiastical colleagues see the situation as one in which an individual, Joan, is challenging the authority of the Church. They see the Church as representing the authority of God, as the guardian of public morals and defender of the faith, fighting against heresy. And they also in varying degrees see their job as being to rescue Joan's soul from damnation by persuading her to accept the Church's assessment of her 'voices'.

Joan, on the other hand, perceives her voices as emanating from the Archangel Michael, St Margaret and St Catherine under direct command from God, whose authority cannot be contested. She sees herself also as a loyal and obedient member of the Church who is obliged nevertheless to trust her angelic voices.

The ecclesiastical officers set a high value not only on obedience to the authority of the Church as represented by themselves, but also on acceptance of the rightness of their judgement as against the rightness of any individual Christian's judgement. Joan attaches an equally overriding value to faithfulness to her angelic messengers and their commands. She is not strictly a member of an identifiable cultural group; but she does nevertheless represent an outlook that is characteristic of some sub-cultures today.

None of the characters in the scene are able to understand the outlook of the other side. Both sides feel threatened at the very deepest level, and each side's perception of the situation seems absurd, even unintelligible, to the other. But the sense of threat relates on each side to their deeply felt and fundamentally inarticulate value commitments: the Bishop's threat to Joan's faithfulness to her angels and her inner vision, and Joan's threat to the Church's interpretation of the Christian faith and the maintenance of ecclesiastical order.

Activity 3: Research and discussion Picture yourself *either* as a teacher *or* as a student engaged in a group discussion of the trial of Joan of Arc. What arguments would you expect to be advanced by the different members of the group?

CULTURE CLASHES IN A RADICALLY CHANGING WORLD

We have looked at a culture clash facing a missionary in present-day Africa, at one in Judea at the time of Jesus, one in the medieval Christian world, and one in the industrial sphere, which all showed the immense power of any culture in influencing its members, and the strength of its resistance to change. Today there is one which faces every society as it copes with the acceleration of economic, social and political development within its own borders. This is the conflict between those who believe in a predominantly 'technocratic' or impersonal technological approach to large-scale social and economic problems and those who believe that the culture of the community itself, with its characteristic scale of values, ought to be at the centre of the planners' attention. The former tend to handle such problems as soil erosion or overpopulation in terms of material and financial objectives and resources; the latter tend to begin from a consideration of the way of life of the community concerned, and to hinge their calculations of objectives and resources on that aspect.

We need now to put the basic concept of a culture clash and the associated conflicts of values into the wider context of the large-scale changes taking place in present-day societies everywhere.

The immense growth of city populations, with a correspondingly huge acceleration in transport and communication services, has resulted in acute problems of urban administration in every part of the world. International relations have become a new focus of concern to multitudes of people, partly because of the threat of nuclear warfare, and because of the desperate poverty and indebtedness of many developing countries. The explosion of new knowledge and new technology in the academic and industrial worlds presents a challenge to traditional authorities, whether governments or employers or parents and teachers. This often includes a rejection of traditional values, which in some cases has led to a powerful backlash from a traditional culture (e.g. in Iran).

Moreover, the intensity of social upheaval, the confusion caused by culture clashes and the scale of possible disaster represent profound changes in the social context within which any Church leader now spends a working life. Traditional value systems can no longer be taken for granted.

Activity 4: Research and discussion Select what you regard as two major social changes that have been taking place in your country in the last twenty years. Write about 300 words on how these have affected you, your family and your Church.

IMPLICATIONS FOR TERTIARY EDUCATION

Church leaders are always likely to find themselves working at the boundary between different cultures. They may be Christian evangelists working in an area where the prevailing outlook is that of, say, militant Islam; or graduates from a professional background working among people suffering the deprivations of a shanty town in Latin America or the slum areas of an industrial city in Britain. They may be theologians from one Asian country teaching in a university in another, where they not only encounter an unfamiliar national culture, but need to adapt to a religious background of, say, Buddhism or Shamanism or Shinto rather than Hinduism or Roman Catholic Christianity. They may be pastors from one African traditional culture working among members of a very different tribal grouping—or even Church workers from one denomination who find difficulty in co-operating with members of another, because the two denominations represent conflicting Christian traditions and different sub-cultures within the same country. The possible variations are endless.

Christian leaders today need to be sensitive to the indications of different cultural assumptions, and question the validity of their own perceptions and values; or as Paulo Freire pithily expresses it, they must re-examine themselves constantly. Some may even experience the clash of opposing cultures and contrasting priorities of values within themselves. People in developing countries especially experience this inner conflict, having perhaps grown up in an extended family in a rural environment, and then moved to (say) a civil service job in a city, where the prevailing outlook and values contrast sharply with those they acquired as they grew up. Even at the simplest level there is a disruption of traditional culture patterns: as a Kenyan lecturer remarked, 'In Kenya we shake hands any time we meet. If you don't shake hands with me, I feel now, why? Some of our educated people are having trouble with their grandmothers and grandfathers: when they come home from a university they don't show that respect, in shaking hands with their grandmother. They are labelled "too proud".' Language differences, too, can cause complications. No two languages have an identical structure, and many misunderstandings and conflicts arise simply from insensitive translation.

Most institutions of tertiary education concentrate upon the sort of objectives we listed on p. 11. Few set out to cultivate an understanding of the subjective factors operating in culture clashes or other conflict situations. They do not regard this as part of their function: the job is left to professional associations, missionary colleges and so on. Nor do they often set out to develop a conscious grasp of the ethical implications of such situations for their students. In fact in many countries, when value questions are raised in an academic seminar, the usual response is to refer them back to the students' own private judgement: both teachers and students feel that this is a sensitive area, and a taboo descends to blanket the subject.

Getting to know one's own unvoiced perceptions and values has another important aspect, which has been explored by the American business consultants Argyris and Schon (34), who make a distinction between 'espoused theories' and 'theories-in-use'. They use the term 'espoused theories' for the ideas and beliefs we acquire from academic studies, and 'theories-in-use' for those which lie behind the actions we actually take. For example, some young Church leaders adopt or 'espouse' theories about how to manage a Church organization so as to get a happy atmosphere, but find that what they actually say or do is quite different from what they intended, and has quite different effects. We saw an example in the staff team who advocated the learning of critical judgement but set examination questions which failed to test it. Theories-in-use tend to be tacit, half-conscious patterns of response and effort, of perception and valuation, whose relation to action is like the relationship of grammar as we use it in everyday conversation to the rules of grammar we are taught in school.

Activity 5: Stop, think and note Give an example from your own experience of having studied the theory of how to do something, and yet found yourself doing something quite different. Try to formulate the theory-in-use behind that action.

In exploring ethical issues we may distinguish three areas. The first is *clarification* of our own values, by which we learn to identify those most powerfully active in ourselves. The second is *analysis* of values, the tracing and disentangling of those which act as driving forces in other people, whether in real life situations or in history or fiction. The third is *critical judgement* of values, by which we define the ethical dimensions of any human situation and examine the validity of the moral decisions taken.

Activity 6: Stop, think and note Describe any course you have *either* attended as a student *or* organized as a tutor in which questions about values have had detailed attention. How was the discussion handled? Was it effective? Explain in what ways it was, or was not, effective.

The problem for tutors is not so much how to incorporate these studies into a curriculum, as how to do so in a way which gives them an existential reality. A purely academic or intellectual approach is unlikely to influence the way students see the social context and ethical implications of their work, or how they approach potential conflict situations. The subject must be handled in a context which *evokes a felt personal response*, yet is not so close to students' personal feelings as to appear threatening. The context or subject matter must also enable them to discover the nature of their own subjective responses, as well as those of other people. An existential impact is essential. In so far as their college community has something of the spirit of *koinonia* referred to on p. 38 tutors will find that these tasks run more smoothly. We return to the down-to-earth practicalities in chapter 12.

IMPLICATIONS FOR CHRISTIANS

As these examples show, any given culture has a profound influence on the way people see the world around them, on how they see other people and situations, and on the priorities they attach to different values. Despite this deep influence, there is still of course an enormous range of variation in their individual personalities and outlooks. My own understanding of Christianity, for example, is profoundly influenced by the Western culture in which I have grown up and developed my thinking. And similarly the understanding of Christianity of any Christian in any part of the world will certainly reflect that person's culture. We have seen how difficult it is for people to get inside the culture of *another* country or society, and it is equally difficult to see and appreciate how far our own assumptions and convictions and carefully worked out views in fact reflect our culture. In approaching questions of doctrine or theology or ethics, Christians in any part of the world have to make strenuous efforts to disentangle from their beliefs those elements which appear to have no validity, or to make no sense, to people from other cultures. This is equally important for Christian tutors, whether they are missionaries or teaching in their own countries, as it is for their students, and indeed for all Christians anywhere. The Korean poet Kim Chi Ha, a Christian imprisoned for protesting against government oppression, has crystallized these experiences in one vivid note:

> ... This peninsula [Korea] is filled with the clamours of grieved ghosts. It is filled with the mourning noise of *han* of those who died from foreign invasion, wars, tyranny, rebellion, malignant diseases and starvation. I have wanted my poems to be the womb of the sounds, the transmitter of the *han* and of a sharp awareness of the historical tragedy. A commentator has been moved to ask me, 'If this is what *han* is, can Christians who have not heard it communicate the Gospel in Korea? Can they speak to the hearts of Koreans?' *Quoted in C. S. Song.* (35)

Thus we see that the contextual or 'existential' theology, discussed in chapter 4 calls not only for an interplay between experience (or action) and reflection, but a critical awareness of the culture which influences our acting and thinking. A white woman student doing her training as a missionary in Southern Africa has emphasized this point:

> ... I heard about a course in language learning which happens in the context of living in the community whose language one is learning. ... So here I am in X ... My home is with a widow, who has three of her five children living with her. ... My hostess is very poor. ... We live in a three-roomed shack. The three boys have one single bed in the kitchen, and she and I share a double bed in her room. She rises at 3.30 a.m., leaving at 4.20 for work. She only gets back at 5.30 p.m. The oldest (13 years) son is responsible for cooking and cleaning. There is mostly just bread, mealie meal, black tea and sugar in the house. She brings meat and vegetables about three times a week. I am learning ingenious ways of washing my whole body in two inches of water in a small laundry bowl. ... All these things have helped me to become a part of this home and community. I have so valued being included in discussions between the women, of their lives and loves, their trials and their dreams, and of their experiences in their relationships to the Lord. ... After a week of constantly making efforts to respond to these very extroverted people, and caring enough to learn not to say or do things wrongly, I hit the second phase of culture shock, where all ... became too much ... and the tears just started and I couldn't stop them. I just longed for familiar routines. ... But the next day was peaceful ... and I was renewed. 'Perhaps the most significant aspect of the informal education [we receive in our culture] is the conviction that the Western world is significantly superior to the so-called Third World; in some way material progress has been equated with corresponding degrees of human happiness' (*Nida*). It is only living here now that I can begin to get a glimmering of understanding this statement. I feel in myself how extremely difficult it is to break down our assumptions, in so far as they are wrong. Before I was given this opportunity to see from a different perspective, I would simply not have comprehended that these Western beliefs may be questioned. ... I do not think we have realized our own levels of poverty; our Western poverty of spirituality, of love, of community ... the pervasive 'identity crises', depressions and the geographical and mental searching journeys so many go on, are rarely perceived as symptoms of a cultural malady.

We may also detect characteristic features of modern Western culture in the case studies already quoted. Dr Krass's description of Tandara (pp. 32–33) refers to his typically Western assumption that the villagers saw themselves as individuals conscious of their separate identity and their right to make their own decisions, especially on so personal a matter as conversion. The trial scene from *Saint Joan* (pp. 36–38) shows Joan as having a similar sense of individual identity and of responsibility to her own conscience.

The case of the American chemical plant illustrates a pattern of authority not in this case shared by the European clients, but nevertheless very general in Western societies: i.e. one in which individuals with special knowledge or skills are expected to contribute to a general debate on that basis, and authority is not strictly hierarchical. The European clients also illustrate another striking feature of Western culture: the competitive striving of individuals in a group to outdo one another. The clash between the impersonal 'technological' approach to agricultural production and the 'environmentalist' approach illustrates another characteristic feature of modern Western culture, namely the expectation that such problems will be handled on the basis of an impersonal technological approach.

One more point. The emphasis throughout this chapter has been on the influence of cultural differences and the need for awareness. But we ought not to under-emphasize the significance of the *shared* features of different cultures. There are those common to human beings everywhere, such as certain aspects of child rearing; and in any two particular cultures there is likely to be some special feature in common, such as similar surroundings. An insight into differences can give stability to a relationship of mutual respect and friendship between people of different cultures.

Thus we have one more key aim for theological education:

Objective 11. To acquire some skill in understanding the characteristic unspoken assumptions of different cultures, that is, the *perceptions* and *value-assumptions* that underlie the behaviour of members of other cultures as well as of their own, and in gaining some insight into the influence of these subjective factors on themselves: in brief, **getting inside cultural assumptions.**

SUMMARY

The first aim of this chapter is to show the powerful influence of the culture of any organization or community to which we belong, on all our behaviour—thought, feeling and action. The second aim follows: to argue the importance of enabling those who are training to be Church leaders to gain an understanding of other cultures and of their own. Five case studies are briefly presented, and a definition of the concept of 'culture' offered. We note the need to distinguish the half-conscious *perceptions* of situations from the *assumptions about values*, and priorities among values, which characterize any given culture. For this, educational methods have to be used which go deeper than the level of abstract reasoning, and elicit felt responses from the students; that is, they must make an existential impact. Finally, we have seen the significance of these considerations for Christians concerned with the communication of their faith to other people.

NOTE ON ACTIVITIES

Activity 1 I would expect you to have written something about a school sports team or a group of close friends in adolescence, or an active committed group in a Church congregation or some other small close-knit body.

7

Students working in isolation

SOME COMMENTS FROM STUDENTS WORKING IN ISOLATION

... Yes, it made me think and I learned a lot. But it did get boring, working on my own. I missed the company, having other students about. *E. Rudd* (36)

... Even a boring lecturer was another person, alive, not just a book or a cassette. (36)

... Whenever I talk about it to anybody I get enthusiastic again. (36)

... I do need a push, and I haven't got that here. (36)

... Although I know self-motivation is supposed to be the great thing, you do need a bit of encouragement from other people. *J. Rudduck* (37)

... I didn't know whether the group was picking out the right topics, the major topics, the major questions, and secondly I didn't know whether we were drawing the right conclusions ... and if you don't know whether [your conclusions] are on the right things coming up for the exams, it may be things that will lose you marks because you've drawn the wrong conclusions. *From a video recording of a small group of students working together in Durham, at a distance from their tutor.*

47

OPEN LEARNING AND DISTANCE LEARNING

Courses of study are usually provided in schools or colleges, and are taught by qualified tutors in classes at fixed times, with access to a library or resource centre. But many would-be students are prevented by circumstances from attending such classes. Some live too far away; some live close enough but other commitments make it impracticable for them to attend at the given times; some find that available programmes do not cater for their needs, either because their interest is too specialized to support a course, or because facilities are lacking; some are prevented by lack of the right entry qualifications. And many lack the necessary financial resources. In all these circumstances individuals have to do a large part of their study on their own. Those who live close to the institution may be able to meet with their tutors outside the normal timetables and to have access to a bookstock, but if they live at a distance this is more difficult. In either case the dominant factor is the isolation of students who have little direct contact with their tutors or with other students. To meet these circumstances 'Open Learning' systems have in recent years been extensively developed, which facilitate the work of students obliged to study largely in isolation. We should not overlook the satisfaction that a keen student can obtain from solitary study, nor the stimulus gained from an alternation of individual study and group discussion. But here we are primarily concerned with the problems likely to arise from sheer isolation.

Most Open Learning courses make special provision in several respects. The learning materials are prepared for this specific purpose, both in their language and presentation and in the media used, in the type of practical activities recommended, and in the methods of assessment. The organizing body also arranges for tutorial assistance and access to a bookstock, for the dispatch of papers and reports, and for the monitoring of the system. And the conditons can of course be adapted in many different ways to the needs of particular groups of students. For example, where students live at a considerable distance from the tutorial centre the pattern of organization needs to be modified. The phrase 'distance learning' is used for arrangements of this sort, which in some countries make extensive use of radio and television, and increasingly employ desk-top computers. The main differences between tutoring in an Open Learning system and customary class teaching are that tutors are no longer the students' chief source of information, and see their students at wider intervals but for more intensive sessions.

Activity 1: Words Explain in your own words the purposes of an 'open learning' system, and explain the difference between 'open' and 'distance' learning systems.

A major problem in both systems is that students working in isolation often suffer considerable strain, being uncertain whether they are correctly understanding or mastering the subject matter, and having to sustain their effort without the stimulus of immediate discussion with a tutor or fellow students.

Activity 2: Stop, think and note Have you ever experienced this kind of strain yourself? What were the circumstances? How did you try to overcome it?

PROVIDING FOR STUDENTS WORKING IN ISOLATION

Ideally, students faced with such circumstances need the following:

(a) An outline of the *content* of the course.

(b) A statement of the further educational purposes, or process-based *objectives*, which the teacher has in mind in providing the course.

(c) A series of *materials* for independent study: 'self-study materials' or an 'Extension course'.

(d) A note of *advice* about improving the effectiveness of their learning.

(e) Practical *exercises* which require them to apply what they are learning to contexts outside the course.

(f) A sequence of *tests* built into the course by means of which they can *gauge their own progress*.

(g) A series of exercises or *tests marked and commented on* by the *tutor*, designed to ensure that the students are gaining an appropriate command of the material, and that they are developing the skills outlined in the statement referred to in (b) above.

(h) The organization of *meetings* between tutor and students on a regular basis.

Of these eight points Item (a) is normal practice. Item (b) we shall discuss in this chapter. Item (c) is discussed in chapter 8 (on materials at a post-secondary level) and chapter 9 (on those at a post-primary

49

level). Items (f) and (g) are covered in chapter 11 and item (h) in chapter 12. Since there is always a good deal of information which students need to commit to memory, some techniques of memorization are described in chapter 13.

As regards item (b), the statement of the purpose of the course, this needs to make clear the range of knowledge, skills, capacities and habits which the course is designed to promote, without daunting students by its complexity or misleading them by over-simplification.

However, to present such a statement may itself create problems, and the newness of such an exercise, and of some of the aims formulated, may provoke queries. Moreover, students themselves vary widely in their purposes and in their abilities. It is highly desirable therefore that the aims should be discussed with students at an early stage in the course, and should be regarded as negotiable.

A STATEMENT OF PURPOSES FOR STUDENTS IN ISOLATION

The following Example is a statement of the eleven objectives presented in chapters 2–6, *in a form which students should readily understand.* (It assumes that tutors preparing for a new TEE course will in fact hold these eleven objectives for that course.) However, tutors will know their own students, and may consider it advisable to change the wording to suit their background. The statement includes suggestions for Exercises based on some of the questions we have already posed in the Activities in previous chapters.

Example 3: A note to students
We hope that through this course you will achieve something of the following objectives, that you will:

Objective 1. Acquire a reasonable command of the basic facts, concepts, techniques and accepted views of the subjects you study; that is, to have this material well stored in your memory: in short, acquiring *basic knowledge.*

Objective 2. Gain a good understanding of your subject discipline. There are three aspects here:

(a) To acquire a framework of ideas or structure of concepts in which the facts, techniques, views, etc. mentioned above have a logical place.

(b) To acquire the ways of thinking and of using evidence that characterize the subjects you are studying.

(c) To develop some skill in applying these ways of thinking in situations directly comparable to those in which you learned them.

These three aspects constitute the subject-discipline, and for convenience this objective may be thought of as gaining a *comprehension of the subject-discipline.*

Exercise 1 Look back at your own schooling. How far did the work consist of memorizing information: for example, learning by heart the names and dates of important people, or the basic facts of historical events? How far did you *understand* what you were memorizing? How did your teachers get you to understand what you were studying?

Exercise 2 'Find out what the staff want you to know and learn it.' Have you been in a school or college where this was the prevailing attitude among the students/pupils? Mention briefly the circumstances.

Objective 3. Acquire a habit of learning for yourself without pressure from your teachers or from an examination, and of working out your own views without depending on your teacher: in short, acquiring a habit of '*self-directed learning*'.

Objective 4. Acquire some skill in expressing ideas or feelings, reporting events, etc., in writing, in speech, in mathematical symbols, in pictures and/ or in other media: in short, developing *communication skills*.

Objective 5. Acquire a capacity for applying what you have learned to entirely new situations, in other words, for solving problems quite unlike the ones you have solved before: developing a capacity for *application in new situations*.

Objective 6. Acquire some skill in analysing (for example) an argument, an article in the press, an interview on television, or a passage in a book; that is, showing how the speaker or writer uses the various ideas, makes logical or illogical connections between them, evokes emotion, etc.: in short, acquiring some skill in *analysing an argument*.

Objective 7. Acquire some skill in devising new concepts, inventing new schemes, producing new plans of action, creating new works of imagination; that is, developing some inventive or creative talent in some area of activity: in short, developing a talent for *invention*.

Objective 8. Acquire some skill in assessing the *quality* of what you have learned or studied: for example, the logical sequence of an argument, the appropriateness of a solution for a problem, the relevance of a discussion to the topic under review. 'Assessing the quality' here means not just *expressing an opinion* but *forming a judgement* based on a consideration of all the relevant factors: in short, developing a capacity for *assessing quality*.

Exercise 3 Look back at your last year at school again. Select a subject of study which you enjoyed and a subject which you disliked. List objectives 1–8 above, and note what your teachers did to promote each aim, first in the subject you liked and second in the one you disliked.

Objective 9. Acquire an existential understanding of academic subject matter (that is, a sense of its becoming part of your everyday mental furniture), and develop a practical judgement of people and situations: in short, developing *existential understanding and practical judgement*.

Exercise 4 Give two or three examples of field work you have been required to carry out as part of an academic course. What aspects of *academic* work did they help you to understand? What part did you think was a waste of time? What real benefit did you gain?

Objective 10. Acquire the skills of effective collaboration with other people, or *team work skills.*

Objective 11. Acquire some skill in understanding the characteristics of different cultures, including your own: in short, *getting inside cultural assumptions.*

Tutors may wish to conclude with notes on the exercises set for students who have been working through the above statement.

Activity 3: Research and discussion You have now read through a modified statement of the educational purposes you might present to your students. This formulation has been written many miles from where you are working. How do you think the various items would be interpreted by your students? Write an assessment of the eleven aims as a whole, commenting particularly on their practicability for *your* students in *their* social circumstances.

Activity 4: Research and discussion The following case study is from H. Taylor, *Tend my Sheep* TEF Study Guide 19 (41).
'For many years Thomas had been a bad husband. He had neglected his wife and children, and wasted most of the family money on drink and gambling. But now he had experienced God's call to change his life. He wanted to become an active member of the Church, and to be a better husband and father. He believed that with God's help he could do this, but was finding his old habits very hard to break. His friends were always asking him to drink with them, and made fun of his desire to be a different person. Supportive counselling would help Thomas to stand firm in his new desire to be better. So the pastor suggested that he should reaffirm his baptismal promises, and told him of the strength he would receive from coming regularly to Holy Communion, and from making new friends within the Church.'
Where do you think your student's training for handling such a task fits into the set of aims quoted? You may find it useful to refer back to chapters 2–6.

NOTES ON ACTIVITIES

Activity 1 On 'open learning' you would need to say something about students who are prevented by circumstances from attending a college course, or there being no course suited to their needs available locally; and hence the idea of a learning guide or Extension Course which would help such students to study effectively in isolation and provide some tutorial guidance. On 'distance learning' you would only need to add that this is for students prevented from attending a set course through being too far away from the teaching centre.

Activity 2 I can only guess at your circumstances. Perhaps you were keen to gain certain qualifications and were prevented from attending the usual course through having a full-time job which you could not give up. Or you lived miles from the nearest educational centre. Perhaps you have obtained information about courses, or even perhaps remained silent, thinking there was no way for you to achieve your aims.

Activity 4 The emphasis here is first on working effectively with other people (Objective 10)—with Thomas himself and his wife, and also with potential friends in the Church congregation; and secondly on understanding the strength of inner habits and motives. (Objective 11), and relating general principles of pastoral work to the setting of a particular community (Objective 9).

8
Self-study materials: post-secondary

FIVE STARTERS FOR SELF-STUDY UNITS

The following tasks are examples of the introductions or starters for five units of work in different self-study courses:

Example 4: A unit on New Testament study Why do we read 1 Corinthians? ... The chief reason why this letter is important to us is because in it Paul showed that the Gospel is true for all people of all times and for all races and under all conditions. Jesus lived and taught in Palestine. Very few of His hearers and followers had received advanced education. Most of them lived in villages or small towns. Most of them were Jews. We today know that what Jesus said and did was true for the whole world and for all ages. But no one could know that at the time. It was necessary for someone to show that it was as true for Jews living in Egypt, Greece, and Italy as it was for the Jews of Palestine whom Jesus Himself had taught. And (what is even more important) someone had to show that it was true for non-Jews as it was for Jews. If no-one had done that, the Christian Church would be no more than a Jewish sect. It was Paul who first did it. This is the main reason why we read 1 Corinthians today. John Hargreaves, *A Guide to 1 Corinthians* TEF Study Guide 17 (4a)

Example 5: A unit on the Church's role in society A fundamental element of the Latin American Church's view of poverty is that it includes not just a lack of material goods but inability to participate fully in social and political life. J. Filochowski and others, *Reflections on Puebla* (43)

To what extent do you consider that 'a lack of material goods' is the *cause* of the 'inability to participate . . .'? Or is the former caused by the latter? Or is there some other connection?

Example 6: A unit on worship The question we have to ask is: How can a pastor help his people, through their common worship, to give spoken and visible expression to the life they have in Christ? . . . If the pastor and the people are from different backgrounds, how can he be sure that what *he* sees as meaningful worship will be meaningful to the people themselves? One answer that has been given . . . is that . . . the liturgies which have been developed once and for all in Europe have universal applicability. . . . Recently, however, many Church people in Africa and Asia have disagreed with this understanding of worship. For worship to be authentic . . . it must be 'indigenous', that is to say it must develop in the culture and in the ways of the Christian community who are doing the worship. Africans cannot be expected to worship according to European ways . . . The problem is, therefore, how to allow a form of worship to develop which will be at one and the same time 'indigenous' (i.e. rooted in the local life of the worshipping community) and also 'catholic' (i.e. rooted in the life and traditions of the whole Christian Church of all times and all places). A. C. Krass, *Go . . . and make disciples* TEF Study Guide 9 (29)

Example 7: A unit on counselling Peter and Mary had attended the same Government secondary school, and become close friends at university. Peter was already promised to marry a young woman from his home area, and his parents and relatives had begun to make plans about the bride-price to be paid. He was not happy with these arrangements because he was in love with Mary and wanted to marry her; however, he did not want to offend his parents. Mary had other difficulties. She liked Peter very much, but she was not happy about his attitude towards her faith. They were both Christians, and Mary was a keen Church member, but Peter had little real interest in the Church. Mary wondered whether she would be wise to marry someone who did not share her faith deeply. Harold Taylor *Tend my sheep* TEF Study Guide 19 (41)

You have recently seen what is meant by 'counselling' in relation to a single individual. How would you suggest that a pastor should approach the problem set by Peter and Mary in the above case study? By what criteria would you judge whether that approach was satisfactory?

Example 8: A unit on Church history An Open University workshop on the Reformation (Francis Clark, *Luther and Lutheranism* (44)) begins with a statement that:
The purpose of this section is to enable you to gather:

(a) An outline of the main facts of Luther's formative years ... up to 1517;

(b) An understanding of his position when he published his Ninety-five Theses in 1517;

(c) An insight into the meaning of the 'evangelical theology' by which he was to give the Reformation its motive force;

(d) Some impression of the character, temperament, and psychological make-up of Luther himself.

The opening section introduces the topic and sets an exercise based on specific reading, to 'write down, giving approximate dates, what you think were the more important events and occupations in Luther's life ... between 1505 and 1517'. A specimen answer is followed by a discussion of the validity of the evidence regarding certain of these events, and then a further exercise on the significance of Luther's 95 theses.

Activity 1: Stop, think and note What do the above five examples of tasks have in common? How do they resemble or differ from the introductions to assignments or units in self-study courses with which you are familiar?

The present chapter is concerned with the design of self-study materials for people who have worked their way successfully through at least a substantial part of secondary education.

Of the five introductions given above, the first is based on a rather arresting question and statement which are likely to have an immediate reality for a theological student. The second also is based on a striking statement calculated to carry a student forward into a detailed examination of the social and religious factors involved. The third raises in simplified but telling form a fundamental question for developing countries outside Europe. The fourth is built on a case study, and the fifth on the setting of a scene revolving round an outstanding individual of very distinctive character. In each case the starter is followed by references to sources which will provide a variety of evidence and arguments from which well-founded views may be worked out.

Some of them also constitute what are sometimes known as 'advance organizers': experiences or reports of experiences or questions which both build on what is familiar and set students' minds working on topics soon to be developed. For instance, Example 4 sets up a question which is likely to overhang the whole of this letter of St Paul's. Example 6 sets up questions which will inspire and permeate the whole unit on forms of worship in developing countries. An advance organizer provides a framework of ideas, an anchor, into which new information can be comfortably fitted and from which it can be comfortably drawn at a later date. It is a way of facilitating that growth from the known into the unknown which weaves the two together into a seamless fabric.

In preparing a self-study or extension course, inexperienced tutors tend to write lengthy pieces of rather technical and indigestible prose—potted lectures rather than guides to study. If we try such materials on a few students we soon find that they do not get much from them. A better method is to turn the procedure back to front, and think in terms of questions or problems that will have some intrinsic meaning, or bite of reality, for the students, into which ideas, facts, evidence etc. can be introduced from various sources. One effect of starting a new phase of work with a specific and striking question is that it stimulates students to search out material that will make an answer possible. This will involve their looking up the various sources provided, assessing their relevance, and assembling the building-blocks of an answer to the question: in short, practising the higher order skills outlined in chapter 2.

Activity 2: Research and discussion Draft two or three questions or short case studies which you could use in opening up a unit in some area of work with which you are involved. What 'academic' content would you intend these openers to lead into? In what way would you be planning to use any of them as advance organizers?

MULTI-MEDIA STUDY MATERIALS

The materials provided for guiding students' work may consist entirely of printed papers and books, or they may include 'multi-media' units also. We use the phrase 'multi-media' units to mean units which include not only printed matter as the medium of communica-tion, but visual media such as pictures, photographs, slides, filmstrips, charts and diagrams; auditory media such as cassettes for playing on tape-recorders; and mixed-media materials like films, slide-tape programmes and video recordings. Suitable material on these lines is available in most countries from Christian bookshops or educational resource centres.

However, many tutors prefer to make their own, ranging from quite simple teaching and learning aids to highly elaborate and specialized programmes. At one end of the scale tutors can devise a multitude of do-it-yourself diagrams and line drawings to use with print-based courses. At the other end are high-level materials, preparation of which calls not only for knowledge of subject matter, but also teaching experience, skill in writing, ingenuity in devising audio-visual materials, technical skills in producing film, slides, audio cassettes etc. and facilities for field testing. Before long it may be practicable to include 'computer programs' which involve students in an exchange of questions and answers. Producing such materials usually requires the co-operation of small teams of specialists: an expert in the subject matter, an experienced tutor skilled in writing in simple and direct language, a librarian familiar with sources of material, a specialist in audio-visual communication. It is not always easy to assemble such teams or to co-ordinate the expertise available. But as the 'hardware' becomes more readily available and the quality of learning materials rises generally, those responsible for producing self-study materials will need to formulate a policy regarding recognition and enlistment of non-teaching staff to collaborate.

> **Activity 3: Words** Explain what is meant by 'audio-visual' teaching materials, 'multi-media' study materials.

CONSTRUCTING A SELF-STUDY COURSE

The essential features required are the following:

(a) The course should be divided into fairly *short units*.

(b) These should include as part of their structure short *'exercises' or 'activities'* designed to engage students in actively debating each fresh point as soon as it is made, checking it back against their own experience or calling for exercise of their own personal judgement. That is, the exercises should promote achievement under the full range of objectives we have considered. As we have seen, there is no reason why the aims connected with critical thinking etc. should only be worked for *after* students have gained a command of Objectives 1 (basic knowledge) and 2 (comprehension of subject discipline). Material promoting the later aims should take its full place in course units throughout the course. For instance, Example 7 can hardly be regarded as 'difficult' in academic terms, but it clearly promotes Objectives 5 (application in new situations) and 9 (existential understanding and practical judgement). Example 8 is designed to prompt students to exercise their judgement on what events counted for most in Luther's development, and on the validity of a historian's comments (Objectives 6, 8 and 9).

(c) These activities or exercises may usefully be followed up at the end of the unit, or perhaps at some later stage, by *notes or suggestions* on what the students might have written or said—similar to the 'Notes on Activities' concluding each chapter of this book.

(d) Opportunities should be provided for *checking back* with students that the materials and their content suit their needs and circumstances. The natural occasion for each negotiation of content is at the group tutorials (see p. 87).

(e) The course *materials*, both the instruction and the activities, should be varied in form and style, making good use of whatever audio-visual techniques, elementary or sophisticated, can be obtained. As facilities become available computer programs should also be brought into use.

Activity 4: Research and discussion What scope do you see for including visual or audio-visual or computer-based materials in the self-study units or extension courses you send out to isolated students? Have you enquired what apparatus is available to them? Have you discovered what visual or audio-visual or computer-based materials available from religious or educational publishers might be suitable or adaptable for inclusion in your self-study or extension courses? What special skills or experience would be available in your institution for producing high quality audio-visual materials?

(f) The course units should in general *open with a problem* which has immediately recognizable reality, presented in a convincing way by means of reports, selected passages from books, case studies, audio cassettes, photographs etc. The five starters cited at the beginning of this chapter illustrate the point.

However, problems that have an 'immediately recognizable reality' can sometimes be difficult to devise. In the study of Church history, for example, the emphasis tends to be severely factual: Where did St Paul go on his second missionary journey? How did it come about that Martin Luther set going the vast movement of the Reformation? The involvement of students tends to be sacrificed to the dating of events or to summarizing arguments. So in an Extension (TEE) course it is essential that the material should be cast in a form which does relate to student's own experience.

One way of doing this is to build the narrative round particular individuals, searching out personal details which will lend credibility to their personalities and actions. Example 8 above builds on the personality of Luther; John Hargreaves uses a similar approach in relation to St Paul in *TEF Study Guide 17* as quoted in Example 4.

Another method is to find points of comparison between the period under study and the present day, or other periods recently studied. And Bible passages can usually be found to endorse or contradict vital ideas of the participants in controversies of earlier periods and can thus be made the basis of Exercises challenging students to think. The *TEF Study Guides* contain abundant examples of this approach.

Tutors may also find difficulty, not only in putting material on a 'problem' footing, but in enabling students to search out materials that will help them to handle the problems offered. Those working at a distance from their college, with limited access to sources of information, will inevitably be more dependent on what the workbook provides.

(g) The course units should also include various types of *tests*: brief self-assessment tests designed to enable students to monitor their own progress; and tests intended for comment and/or assessment by a tutor.

(h) The course materials should be *tried out* on a small scale before being adopted for general use. As shown by the comments quoted on p. 47, students working in isolation sometimes find it difficult to know whether they have grasped the questions or arguments correctly. What is perfectly clear to the writer of an assignment may contain unrecognized obscurities or ambiguities. Field testing is important, even on a minimum scale like showing the first drafts to fellow tutors and a few willing students.

(j) Each unit or section of a unit should conclude with a *summary* of the main ideas, arguments and evidence it has put forward, as has been done in chapters 2–6, which deal with broad general concepts of education in a social context.

(k) Finally, the workbook itself should be made *attractive* to look at and pleasant to handle.

STATING THE OBJECTIVES

In chapter 2 we distinguished between knowledge-based and process-based objectives, and throughout this book we have emphasized the eleven Objectives set out in chapters 2–6, most of which are process-based. However, in some courses, particularly those designed to help students to prepare for formal examinations, it can be helpful to start each assignment or section of a unit by stating its knowledge-based objectives. This statement will be more useful to both tutors and students if it says what students should be able to *do* after completing the unit, rather than what they should *know*. This is not always easy, but it helps if the phrasing is based on verbs which point to *action*, such as 'state', 'describe', 'define', 'translate', 'compare'. For example, the statement for an assignment starting with a task might run as follows:

Example 9 The expected outcome of this assignment is that student(s) will be able to:

(a) explain the meaning of the word 'ministry';

(b) describe several ways in which a pastor should minister to a congregation;

(c) describe three important problems likely to face a pastor on first joining a congregation; and

(d) outline possible ways of dealing with the problems described.

Analysing subject matter and formulating knowledge-based objectives in a precise manner is an art in itself, which we cannot discuss in detail here. Example 8 above quoted a rather similar statement of purposes, but focused on process-based objectives.

Activity 5: Stop, think and note Write what you think you should be able to *do* as a result of your work up to this point in the present chapter.

Activity 6: Stop, think and note Now re-work chapter 7 and the present chapter to this point, and assess how far these units have implemented principles (a)–(k) above, particularly (b), (e), (f) and (g).

HOW TO STUDY EFFECTIVELY

Students will also benefit from guidance on how to study effectively. For example, they might be offered something on the following lines:

Example 10: How to study effectively Individuals vary greatly in what they find to be—for them personally—the most effective ways of studying. But here are some general guidelines which you may find useful:

(a) Get yourself in the right mood for study: the most convenient setting or surroundings, a relaxed frame of mind, reasonable freedom from interruption.

(b) When you read a passage, try to get at the basic ideas, the core of the argument, that the author is offering; try noting them down in your own words. See also if you can recall any first-hand experiences of your own which illustrate or raise questions about the piece you have been reading. Note these and also any other relevant sources. *This paragraph is especially important, and an extra note is added below to explain why.*

(c) At the end of a section see if you can—without looking back—note down the main stages of the argument which it contained.

(d) Check your notes of (c) against your notes of (b) and the passage itself. Correct any mistakes, and improve your original notes by re-classifying the material or translating it into diagrams.

(e) See whether the passage you have been studying prompts any questions. Note these down; note any other ideas you have on the subject.

(f) Read the textbook sections relating to any tests you have done on the subject, whether self-assessment tests or those marked by your tutor, and build into your notes any corrections or clearer statements that you may need.

Additional note on para. (b) above: Some careful observation of the way students study has come up with certain findings. Some students, it seems, dig much more deeply into what they read than others. They search out the inner core of the argument; they look for any personal meaning the material may have for themselves or any relevant first-hand experience; they tend to challenge the ideas they are reading. In contrast to this, others tend to concentrate on separate facts, and to try to memorize the distinct ideas that are included. The former is known as a 'deep' approach to the material, the latter as a 'surface' approach. The following accounts given by two students illustrate the two approaches. [At this point the first and third of the student reports given on pp. 13–14 should be quoted.]

These quotations make it clear that a 'deep' approach will make a much greater contribution than a surface approach, both to the development of critical thinking and to the understanding of any subject. In Bible study particularly we need to gain a thorough understanding of the context in which a given passage was written, and of the lessons it contained for people of that period. We then need to work out in depth the message it may contain for us now, in our own family or community.

This background will enable you to see why para. (b) above has been particularly emphasized.

NOTES ON ACTIVITIES

Activity 1 What the Examples have in common is (among other things) that each asks a question which gives the topic an immediate reality for the student. Assignments or units usually start either with a revision of previous work, or with an explanation of new work or a short statement of the aims of the unit.

Activity 3: Some descriptions similar to those used in the preceding text.

Activity 5: I expect you will have come up with something on the following lines: 'I should be able to:

(a) draft an introduction or starter for any assignment or unit which will have an immediate meaning for my students;

(b) test out the possibilities of including visual and/or audio-visual materials in the self-study documents that I send out to my students;

(c) see what arrangements can be made for small-scale field-testing of the preliminary drafts of those materials;

(d) draft lists of objectives for assignments or units, where appropriate; and

(e) advise my students on how to study most effectively on their own.'

Activity 6: I would expect something on the following lines:

(a), (b), (c), (g), (j): considerable implementation;

(d), (h): not applicable;

(e): little scope for variety of media in this book;

(f): some degree of implementation of this principle.

9

Self-study materials: post-primary

USING PROGRAMMED LEARNING METHODS

In this chapter we are concerned with the design of self-study materials for students with no more than a primary schooling behind them, and possibly not the whole of that. The society in which they live may be a largely non-literate society, and their experience of learning from the printed word may be fairly restricted. The kind of 'starters' offered on pp. 53–55 are too complex and contain too many abstract concepts, to be useful to them. They need materials which use simpler language and are broken down into shorter units, and which build in an immediate use and check-back of the content. Much of the teaching material produced in Latin America, Africa and South East Asia has been based on a Programmed Learning (PL) model (usually referred to in the USA as Programmed Instruction or PI). This shows the following features:

1. The objectives of each unit are defined at the start, as described on p. 60.

2. The course materials consist of a workbook or text, usually in the local language, in which the units of study are no more than 10–12 lines of text.

3. An active response is called for in each unit, which involves writing a few words in reply to a question presented in the unit.

4. The answer to the question presented is contained in the very next unit, so that students receive immediate feedback as to the correctness of their reply.

5. There are periodical meetings, often known as Group Tutorials, of tutors with students, usually in groups of 10–20 members.

6. There may also be occasional questions demanding an active response of a different kind, such as the drafting of a short sermon to be given and discussed at a Group Tutorial, or some simple research, like seeking information on the growth of the local congregation from older members.

7. At the beginning of each Group Tutorial there is a brief test of the students' grasp of what has been studied since the preceding meeting, and after the completion of (say) a 10-week course, a test on the whole course.

The following example, consisting of six 'frames' or small units of text, is from a PL workbook by Jonah Moyo and Grace Holland (51).

Example 11

Week 5: What shall I say about Christ?
Day 4: Men must receive new life.
When we talk to people we must have things ready to say. We have learned three of these. We have learned three verses to show these things.
1. Yesterday we learned Romans 6.23. What big thing can we tell people from this verse? ....

We must tell people that God gives new life. Look what God does. He *gives*.

2. What did we say we must do if someone tries to give us something? We must ....

God does not force us to have new life. We can receive it if we want it. Or we can refuse it.

3. If we want God's gift, what must we do? ....

This is the next big thing we must tell people. Read all the things.
  (1) God gave life to men. Genesis 2.7.
  (2) Men refused life. Romans 3.23.
  (3) God gives new life in Christ. Romans 6.23.
  (4) Men must receive new life. John 1.12; 1 John 1.9.

4. What is the fourth big thing we must tell people? ....
....

5. What two verses can we use to show this? (1) ....
  (2) ....

We must help people to understand well. If they want a new life in Christ, they must receive it. But how can they receive it? The Bible tells us how. We must believe and confess. John 1.12.

  But to all who received him, who believed in his name, he gave power to become children of God.

6. When people receive Christ, what must they do in His name?

....

We must tell people to receive by *believing*. They must believe that Jesus died for their sins. Then He gives them new life. He makes them His children. Read the verse again. John 1.12.

  But to all who received him, who believed in his name, he gave power to become children of God.

7. Look carefully at this verse. Can a person who does not receive Jesus be a child of God? ....

The Bible also says that we should *confess*. We have learned that sin brings death. If we want new life, we must get rid of sin. Here is a verse which tells us how to get rid of it. 1 John 1.9.

  If we confess our sins, he is faithful and just, and will forgive our sins and cleanse us from all unrighteousness.

8. From this verse, who takes away sins? ....
9. What must we do if we want Him to take our sins away? ....
....

Activity 1: Research and discussion Fill in the answers to the questions in Example 11. How can you tell whether you are right or not? To what extent do the authors of the text ask the students to check the lesson against their experience? To what extent do the authors ask them to exercise their personal judgement, based on their experience?

We may notice in Example 11 that the workbook quoted rarely asked students to check the text against their own experience or to exercise their judgement beyond the correct grasp of the text. Its main objective was that students should *assimilate the pieces of information presented in the text*, in working their way through it. *The questions themselves* do not call on students to think about their own experience, nor to compare what they read with views they have built up in their daily living, nor to reflect on the meaning of what they have lived through. This aspect of the work is expected to be catered for in the Group Tutorials, where the main task will be to discuss the bearing of the week's study on daily life, and to interpret what the students have read in the light of their everyday problems in the community. But as we have seen (pp. 57–58), activities should *themselves* be designed to generate thinking that serves Objectives 3 (self-directed learning), 6 (analysing an argument), and 9 (existential understanding and practical judgement). If students are to develop a habit of reflecting on their experience and interpreting it in the light of their reading, and of their discussion and thinking, then we need to *build into their routine study the sort of activities that call for that kind of thinking.*

If on the other hand our chief concern is that students should amass a store of factual information—perhaps of the Bible or of Christian doctrine—then the basic PL technique is well suited to that objective. This approach is widely adopted in colleges where students' academic proficiency is tested by the traditional form of examination, and the interplay between academic study and everyday experience is considered to be adequately catered for in tutorial discussions.

Certainly the basic PL techniques listed as items 2–4 on p. 63 are an effective way of enabling people to assimilate printed information. Certainly, too, students training for leadership in the Church, whether ordained or lay, do need to take in a good deal of factual information about the Bible and the Church itself, as well as learning how to relate points of doctrine to real life experience. Programmed texts, being very precise, can avoid emotionally loaded phrases, and so can be very useful in politically sensitive situations.

ENQUIRY-BASED WORKBOOKS

The question is, then, how to adapt the customary PL pattern so that it both enables students to assimilate information, and also prompts them to exercise a personal judgement and reflect on their real-world experience.

In Example 11 the extent to which students were referred back to their own experience and judgement was very restricted. On the other hand, as we saw, both effort and imagination were used to simplify the language and ideas.

The following example is from another workbook, this time on the Old Testament, by John Simalenga (52).

Example 12
The Message of the Prophets
In traditional African societies there are specialists called 'Seers'. These were people who could see beyond ordinary people, and give an analysis of life events. However, these specialists did not claim any direct guidance from God, but through 'mediums' (individuals held to be channels of communication between the earthly world and a world of spirits).

The prophets of the Old Testament were great religious thinkers and preachers who spoke directly for God. They spoke on a wide range of issues: (a) Social, (b) Economic, (c) Political, (d) Religious, warning people of all ranks: lay, priests, and leaders, of God's judgement if they departed from the just and righteous ways of God.

They analysed their messages in many ways: visions, dreams, listening to God's Spirit, and by interpreting the signs of their times of history (or conditions of life) of which they were a part.

Suggested questions for discussion in groups
1. What do you think about a religious leader speaking on political issues?
2. Do you think it is possible to play the role of Old Testament prophets today?
3. How did the prophets get their message?
4. What is your experience of visions or dreams?
5. What other questions do you have?

Activity 2: Research and discussion On what basis of experience and thought would you wish to discuss Question 1 in Example 12? And *in the culture to which you belong* what scope do you think there would be for an answer to Question 4? What talents or skills will you need to exercise in answering these questions?

The following section of a unit is from a third workbook, by Rosario Batlle (53).

Example 13
TWO INTIMATE FRIENDS OF JESUS (Martha and Mary)
Bible Reading: Luke 10.38-42; John 11.1–45.

Introduction: This Unit will deal with the following:
1. Martha,
2. Mary,
3. The relationship between Jesus and the two women (a),
4. The relationship between Jesus and the two women (b),
5. What Jesus expected of Martha,
6. Doing and Being (a),
7. Doing and Being (b),
8. Review.

The Aim of this Unit: After studying this Unit you should be able to describe in your own words what Jesus's words 'Mary has chosen the better thing, and I will not take it away from her', mean for your own life as a Christian.

1. Martha
We can see from the biblical reading that Martha is very conscious of her duty as hostess to guests in her house. She is *self-confident* as she manages the work in the kitchen. She was the 'perfect woman' according to all the customs of that day. There seems to be some sisterly rivalry or she would not have asked Jesus to take sides ('Make Mary come and help me'). She would have merely asked Mary to come and help.

Perhaps Martha was the *outgoing, active, and managerial type (a natural organizer)*, making sure that everything was in order. In the story in John 11, we also see Martha as a woman who has a very good *intellectual* mind. She is able to maintain her freedom of thought. She is sceptical about Lazarus coming back to life—(John 11.39). She is also able to discuss theology with the Son of God (John 11.21–27). The *domestic-type* Martha is discussing about who Jesus is and understanding what she is talking about. She is a woman of great *faith* for she believes that whatever Jesus asked of God, God would grant (v. 22). Even in our days many women identify with Martha. The kitchen and the home is where women spend most of their lives, doing the same functions in the Church also, even though they are gifted with a keen mind and able to discuss matters about God. Martha symbolizes the *traditional* woman's position—tending, serving, nurturing.

Questions suggested for discussion in groups
1. Describe in your own words the type of woman Martha was, naming some of her characteristics.
2. Can you explain why she was upset with her sister?
3. Do you blame her for feeling like that? Why?
4. Do you know many women who are Martha-type in your culture?
5. Do you expect them to feel like Martha when left alone in the kitchen? Why?
6. Would you personally feel like that in in the same situation? Why?
7. Can you remember feeling like that? When and why?
8. Do you have any other question concerning frame 1?

[There follows a corresponding picture of Mary's character, with questions for discussion.]

In Example 13 we see work of quite a different kind from that quoted earlier. There is a direct comparison between the two women's actions, the Jewish culture of that period, and the culture to which the students belong. The questions refer to the text but go well beyond the text, throwing the students back on *their* experience, on *their* views about the Gospel in relation to their own society, and on *their* moral judgement about the place of women in the community. However, we may also notice that some of the questions (2, 4, 8) could be answered with a plain 'yes' or 'no'. In chapter 12 we will be looking at the way questions can be formulated to stimulate thinking and discussion.

Three questions follow: how far should contextualization be carried? How can these ideas be applied to training in prayer for post-primary students? And what are the implications for Bible study for these students?

HOW FAR CONTEXTUALIZATION?

The question then arises: how far is it right for a workbook to reach out into what might be considered non-Church enterprises? One Christian organization in Kenya, for example, has commissioned a series of workbooks on primary health care, placing pre-natal and post-natal care in the setting of a Christian community. One African diocese provides three-day workshops for ordinands in training, on the way in which local development projects—sinking a well, establishing a primary school—can be organized as an activity *of a Christian community*. These questions are matters which must depend in part on local economic conditions and local political practice, but chiefly on the aims and priorities of the Christian community which is organizing the Extension courses. Paulo Freire insists that the poor and dispossessed need to learn to believe in themselves, in their own ability to think and speak for themselves. As an African tutor with TEE experience said:

> ... I very much tried to follow Freire's principles and it worked very very well ... It was a kind of liberating force. They could speak about things that they did not speak about on other occasions.They had very deep questions in areas of theology and even politics and social order and wanted to know what Christ said about all these issues. It was a kind of letting out all that they had in their minds. Simply airing all their feelings did a lot for them. It was like coming out of themselves and becoming new people. We got so much together. They still come to see me.

If this aim is given a high priority, then the development aspects may well be given a more central place in the workbooks.

TRAINING IN PRAYER AND SPIRITUALITY

It is essential to make adequate provision for growth in prayer and spirituality. In applying the ideas set out above for post-primary groups an experiential basis is necessary, and the following sequence illustrates an approach:

Example 14
Exercise 1 Note down two or three occasions when you have prayed with a bursting heart.

If your experience has been like that of many Christians, these occasions will have been of two kinds. On the one hand there will have been the times when something of tremendous joy and delight has happened and your heart is bursting with the wonder of it, and your prayer is a shout of heartfelt praise and thanks to God, perhaps the more intense for being shared with other members of your family or your community. On the other hand there will have been occasions when some fearful danger has threatened you or your loved ones, or some dreadful disaster has overtaken them, and you pray desperately for God's help to avert the danger or to make the disaster less catastrophic than it has at first appeared.

Exercise 2 Read Psalms 142 and 145. How far has the writer of these poems captured *your* experience?

Such an introduction will have an immediate reality for most Christian students, at whatever level. It must then be followed by training in regular habits of prayer. For example we may go on to:

Exercise 3 Note down a fault or weakness in yourself which causes you to repeatedly hurt or injure somebody to whom you are deeply attached, such as a husband or wife, or a parent, or a child. How do you feel when you have yet again caused that person pain and sorrow? Now read Luke 18. 9–14. How do you think the tax collector felt? How was it that the Pharisee did not feel the same as the tax collector?

If we read some of the writings of great Christian saints of past history we find them lamenting the extent to which they have again and again committed offences against God: they have felt trapped in sinfulness which they can never overcome by their own efforts. Here is a passage from the autobiography of St Teresa, who was born in Spain in 1515—nearly 500 years ago (60). She was a very bright and enterprising child: at the age of six she persuaded a brother to run away with her to seek martyrdom at the hands of the Arabs, since this would (she thought) get them to heaven by a short cut. Luckily the children were seen by an uncle just outside their town. At the age of seventeen she had a serious illness, and was plagued with ill health for twenty years. As she said of herself, 'This body of mine has never brought me anything but ill!' She became a nun at the age of twenty, in a convent which was very lax and where she had a highly sociable and entertaining life, full of gossip and gaiety. But she gradually felt more and more drawn to a life of prayer and austerity and in her autobiography her devotion to God and her love for Jesus shine through. She wrote about this period of her life:

'I led a very wretched life, for as I prayed I gained a clearer knowledge of my faults. On one side God called me, and on the other I followed the world. All divine things gave me great pleasure; yet those of the world held me prisoner. ... Oh if only I could tell of the situations from which God delivered me, and how I plunged into them again and again. Oh Lord of my soul, how can I extol the mercies you showed me in those years? Indeed, at the very times when I most offended you, you quickly prepared me by a very great repentance to taste your gifts and graces.'

And again: 'Once, my Lord, it seemed to me impossible that I should forsake you utterly. But now that I have forsaken you so often I cannot help being afraid. Whenever you withdraw only a little way from me, I immediately fall to the ground. May you be blessed for ever since, although I have forsaken you, you have never so utterly forsaken me as not to raise me up again by continually giving me your hand.'

At that time Teresa learned to pray regularly, using some book about the Christian life, or a part of the Bible, such as the Psalms: 'I never ventured to start praying without a book. I tried as hard as I could to bring the presence of Jesus Christ, our Lord and our God, into my heart; and this was my method of prayer.' (61)

Exercise 4 Read through Psalm 73. Does any verse in particular strike home? If so, do not neglect the opportunity to express that feeling in prayer. It is very useful to start a journal or diary in which to note any short passage which has that special quality of reinforcing your sense of the reality of God's presence and love. You will sometimes find when you make such an entry that you wish to explain to yourself a little of what you have felt, or to talk to a friend about it.

In Example 14 we may notice the use made of the Bible as a resource on which to build prayer, and of the vivid personal reports of a saint.

IMPLICATIONS FOR BIBLE STUDY

The workbooks rightly make continual use of Bible passages. As these examples make clear, there is nothing to stop the authors of workbooks adapting the Bible study to the educational level of the students, whatever that may be. They can distinguish between the various kinds of writings contained in the Bible: records of real people, prophecies, parables, legends, devotional poetry and so on. They can explain in concrete terms the context of a given episode in the Jewish society of the time. And they can bring home the meaning or message that a passage may have for themselves and their own family or community.

A TEE ORGANIZATION FOR POST-PRIMARY GROUPS

Any form of open or distance learning calls for a fairly elaborate organization. The Directors or Co-ordinators of districts or diocesan areas will probably have to train Group Leaders to conduct the regular weekly discussion meetings or Group Tutorials. As we have seen, discussion leaders and students alike may not easily adjust to the new system. Tutors who have to establish or develop TEE centres will therefore need to set up suitable training courses. Much group work will be needed to enable the new Group Leaders to experience and absorb their new roles. If a tape recorder is available it can be useful to lead and record a sample discussion, and analyse the recording. Group leaders will benefit from hearing and analysing their own efforts.

Tutors and Group leaders will also have to select suitable workbooks for the students, and in some situations may have to write them themselves or train others to do so. Agustin and Rosario Batlle provide a three-month course in Kenya for this purpose, in four stages. In the first, which is held in Nairobi, the trainees analyse existing texts and learn the principles involved; they may try their hands at writing. Next, they spend three weeks taking part in TEE classes in the rural areas of Kenya. Then, on returning to Nairobi, they launch into systematic practice in writing, perhaps through translating existing material into their own vernacular. Finally they will become involved in preparing new workbooks based on their intimate knowledge of their own local culture. These courses are held under the auspices of the Organization of African Instituted Churches, but the Batlles are also engaged in holding meetings in various parts of Africa to explain the aims of the work and help to set up new centres in other African countries.

A weakness of some existing TEE schemes is the assumption that the students can only do their TEE work in isolation in their own homes during the week. In many rural areas they will, it is true, be too far separated from fellow students to collaborate outside the Group Tutorials. But in towns some students may be living close enough to one another to discuss assignments together or carry out small projects jointly. In chapter 10 we look at examples of modest schemes which three or four students could profitably undertake together during the week.

NOTES ON ACTIVITIES

Activity 1 You can tell whether each answer is correct by reading the next frame. The text rarely includes questions that tap the readers' experience or call for exercise of a personal judgement.
Activity 2 Question 1 clearly calls for a good deal of thinking about the role of Church leaders in commenting on public affairs. You will need to have some sense of the realities of political life, as well as a shrewd moral judgement.

10
Practical projects for individuals and groups

SOME EXAMPLES OF PRACTICAL PROJECTS

Chapter 8 began with examples of tasks suitable for introducing units of a course. Here are three more:

Example 15
Visit the building(s) where your Church congregation (a) holds services, and (b) holds meetings of committees and other groups, and draw a plan to scale. How do you see the role of these buildings in serving the community in which your congregation forms part? If you think the buildings could be made more suitable, design alterations, or a new building, giving the reasons for your proposals. When you have sketched out your report, get two or three of your friends together and discuss it with them. What differences of opinion were there? Had you overlooked any important aspects? If so, can you throw any light on what unconscious assumptions led you to do so?

Example 16
Make a list of the different groups of which your society is composed and divide them into three sorts: (a) groups who are related through family ties or marriage; (b) groups of people related to one another because they live in one village or town; and (c) groups formed for a special purpose, e.g. work or play. Does your society also have other sorts of groups, e.g. based on age or sex? Look at your lists and think of those who are Christians. From which of the groups you have listed do they mostly come, or from all groups

equally? If there are several Christian denominations in your area, are they related to the groups which make up your society, in the same way, or in different ways? What reason can you suggest for the answer? What differences, if any, are there between the approaches used by the various denominations in ministering to their congregations?

Example 17
Arrange to visit an organization such as a shop, or a workshop that produces some goods, or a school, and ask the head of the organization to be kind enough to allow you to observe the way the organization works, and to answer some questions about it. Write a report on your visits, noting (a) the purpose of the organization; (b) the number of people employed; (c) what these people do; (d) who the clients are; (e) how the senior people in the organization maintain control of it, how they exercise authority; and (f) the climate of opinion and relationships in the organization. Please remember to give your thanks at the end.

These three examples of practical projects all involving field work; i.e. they combine academic study with first-hand experience or observation in the student's own neighbourhood. The first calls for a visit to a building; the second for enquiries among people in the area, with reflection on the knowledge acquired then or earlier. The third involves a more formal approach and a more elaborate study. The use of practical projects (see ch. 4) has spread widely in recent years. They give students an opportunity to build their academic studies on first-hand experience, and to interpret their first-hand experience in the light of what they learn from academic study. This 'experiential' learning helps them to establish existential links between everyday living and academic thinking. The 'Activities' or 'Exercises' inserted in the text are themselves forms of 'practical work'. The phrase 'experiential learning', here used to mean that learners are directly in touch with the realities being studied, is also used in a narrower sense, to mean 'knowledge and skills acquired through life and work experience and study *before* entry to any course'.

Activity 1: Stop, think and note In the light of chapter 4, note what you would hope students might gain from each of the above projects, in terms of (a) a clearer grasp of academic concepts; (b) a clearer grasp of principles of professional action; and (c) personal development and social skills.

The three projects described could be undertaken by individuals or by small groups. Students working at a distance from their institution are often too isolated to engage in group projects. But where students are able to find three or four friends with whom to form a working team the rewards are great.

Activity 2: Words Explain in your own words what may be meant by 'experiential learning'. Give two or three examples from your own experience.

MARRYING FIELD WORK TO ACADEMIC CONCEPTS

It is not always easy to ensure that students succeed in integrating field experience with their academic study. Tutors may lack personal knowledge of the place where students are gaining the experience; and workplaces vary in what they can offer: people change, organizations change, circumstances change. Sometimes failure is due to inadequate preparation of students before they embark on field experience. They may carry out a practical project as instructed, but have no clear understanding of how it relates to their academic studies, or will help to prepare them for their future job.

If any kind of practical field work is to be included in a course, there are four essential steps tutors will need to take:

1. clarify their own thinking as to what learning they wish the students to gain, both in terms of an academic syllabus and in personal development;

2. formulate the aims of the work in terms of problems or questions to which students should be finding answers (see pp. 20, 21, 56);

3. obtain detailed information about the workplace or other organizations students may research, if possible by a personal visit: this means getting in touch with some responsible person at the workplace and explaining the objectives they have in mind, and hence agreeing on what the student can be expected to do and learn;

4. prepare students for the project by briefing them beforehand, checking their progress during it, and reviewing their interpretation of the experience after the exercise.

The briefing means giving students the necessary information about the scene of their work. It must include a detailed explanation of what they are expected to do, what academic aspects they should focus on, what personal and social skills they may expect to develop, and what difficulties they are likely to encounter. Students find it useful to have a note of practical advice and a check-list of questions to keep in mind before going out on field work. The review stage, or 'debriefing', should include both a systematic report by the students, either written or oral, on the various aspects of the exercise, and an opportunity for the tutor to discuss the significance of the experience with them. For example, did individual students all get the same subjective impressions from the experience? Do they agree on the interpretation of those impressions? How did that interpretation fit in with their academic studies? Did the experience throw any light on their personal problems in living a Christian life? If a tape-recorder is available it is worth recording the debriefing sessions, and then replaying them to check the effectiveness of a discussion in which they all have a personal stake.

Other practical projects can be of many kinds, ranging across all the subjects of a college curriculum, but the same precautions are needed as with field work schemes. If individual students are invited to offer their own proposals for projects, tutors need to ensure that these are of more or less equal difficulty; and they should be based on first-hand information rather than information from books. Students must be asked to make clear the *purposes* for which projects they propose are designed, and must also understand the criteria by which they are to be assessed.

WORK EXPERIENCE AND PLACEMENTS

Work experience and job placements are an important part of most kinds of professional training today, and are equally useful for students training to be Church leaders. Advice about the sort of experiential knowledge and practical judgement they may acquire in this context might include such objectives as the following:

(a) that they should experience a range of tasks in the parish or Church to which they are attached, and get a sound understanding of the whole organization and its relation to their formal studies (part of our Objectives 5 and 9);

(b) that they should develop such skills as learning to work closely with others, of whatever status (our Objective 10);

(c) that they should develop their skills in expressing themselves clearly and effectively (our Objective 4);

(d) that they should develop habits of dependability, punctuality, politeness, etc. in their workplace (our Objective 10 again);

(e) that they should attempt to assess their level of skill and personal development in the light of that experience, with its implications for their own future job (part of our Objectives 9 and 11).

Students should also be required to keep a diary or journal in which to record not only events, but their own responses and the comments of their supervisors.

As in the case of field work, briefing needs to be full and precise. We could hardly expect students to gain a full and detailed understanding of the objectives or the actual effect on themselves of such work experience if they received for their placement no more than the instructions described by one tutor as follows: 'We [the staff] tell them they are going into a parish to work with a vicar. [We say] "Do what he tells you to do. Keep a diary. Make sure that when you visit someone you note in your diary what the problems are and how you try to solve them." That is all we say.'

Activity 3: Stop, think and note Cast your mind back to any placement, whether in a city parish or a rural congregation, which you may have undertaken as part of an academic course or professional training. What aspects of your *academic* studies did it help you to understand? What part if any did you think was a waste of time? In so far as it was part of a theological or pastoral training, what benefit did you get in terms of a deeper understanding of how Christians should live? of the obstacles Christians face? of the difficulties *you* find in leading a Christian life? (Compare ch. 4, Activity 7).

The debriefing stage offers considerable opportunities for tutors to open up with students the implications of their experiences in terms of understanding organizations and communities, and—perhaps especially—of looking at the different ways in which authority is exercised and the different structures or chains of authority they have encountered. Extremely important questions arise about the ways in which Christians think of authority, and the influence of the past or existing culture of a community or organization on the style of authority that is acceptable to its members as well as conforming to a Christian view. Another aspect of workplace life worth discussing is the diversity of ways in which organizations and communities handle processes of change, whether imposed by external forces such as economic circumstances or government policy, or generated from within themselves. All these follow-up topics can profitably be handled on a small-group basis. Where feasible, students' reports on their job placements can usefully be presented in the form of an exhibition, for the information of their fellow students as well as placement supervisors.

Activity 4: Research and discussion Draw up a note of advice for students embarking on a one-month placement in a parish, including a check-list of what they should aim to do and to find out.

Field work projects and work placements must, in the early stages of development, be planned in great detail and carefully managed. But at a more advanced stage they may be given a more ambitious scope, on the lines, perhaps, of the scheme decribed on pp. 22–24, lending some justification to Paulo Freire's comments:

> ... In problem-posing education, men develop their power to perceive critically *the way they exist* in the world *with which* and *in which* they find themselves ... problem-posing education regards dialogue as indispensable to the act of cognition which unveils reality ... [Here] we find two dimensions, reflection and action, in such radical interaction that if one is sacrificed ... the other immediately suffers. ... Dialogue is an existential necessity. ... [It] cannot, however, exist in the absence of a profound love for the world and for man. (7)

ROLE PLAYING

Another useful form of practical work, particularly for promoting objective 9 (existential understanding and practical judgement), is role playing. This can be done in various ways. One way is to write a script for a dialogue between (say) a father and a rebellious teenage son, to illustrate a particular kind of tension or relationship, which two students then read and act out for the group to comment on and discuss.

An alternative is to write instructions for two people to behave in certain ways, and get two students to act the parts. In this case neither knows exactly what he himself will say or how the other will respond. For example, one student plays the part of an embittered agnostic on his death-bed, or a newly-converted parent whose only child has been killed in an accident, and the other the part of a minister attempting to make a persuasive case for a Christian view.

In a more elaborate exercise several people are allocated parts, perhaps a young married couple, the parents of one partner, their parish priest or a Church elder, and a local government officer. Such cases grade into large-scale 'academic games' or 'simulations', based perhaps on some crisis situation in an imaginary Church congregation or village community. These would involve more complex emotions and difficult decisions, and might last several hours.

Here too, tutors need to have a very clear idea of the concepts they wish students to grasp, and the sort of spontaneous responses and emotions the students are likely to empathize with, and which the play will help them to understand. Students easily get carried away by their roles, and the feelings of anger, frustration or distress aroused can be disturbingly powerful. Sometimes the patience and support of the whole group may be needed to ease individual role-players back into the real-life situation.

COMMUNICATION SKILLS AND THE ART OF REPORTING

The development of communication skills (Objective 4) is of enormous importance, and both tutors and students need to be clear about what they are, and are not, trying to do. The communication skills exercised in role-play work are rather different from those involved in field work: e.g. listening attentively to what people say, clarifying one's own thoughts and responses, conveying just the shade of meaning one intends in words as well as in the expressions of face and voice.

There are many different circumstances in which students have to produce reports. The sort of 'Activities' given in this book require short reports of experiences or views. Tutors may call on individual students to write reports of jointly conducted field work schemes, or of conclusions reached in small-group exercises. Or they may be required to preach sermons or give religious instruction during a job placement with a congregation. The following is an example of basic guidelines for students producing reports, particularly useful perhaps for those who work in isolation.

Example 18
1. Jot down in a random list very brief notes of *all* the ideas and pieces of information you think might be recorded in your report. In preparing a more formal essay this may be a miscellaneous list of facts, ideas, thoughts and impressions, together with various questions which have come into your mind.

2. Put these into a suitable order. The order will to some extent depend on what you are reporting. It may be simply the order of certain events as they occurred; or you may have to start by explaining how a project came to be planned. In some cases—e.g. in addressing a meeting—you may need to start with a striking remark or quotation which will immediately grip the audience's attention.

3. Mark off your material in distinct sections, with a sub-heading for each,

ensuring that each general idea or view is clearly linked with its supporting evidence. The first three stages require no connected writing or anything like an essay: they are an essential preliminary for any report, whether written or oral.

4. Write in as clear and simple language as possible what you are trying to say.

5. Many people find it useful to adopt a systematic approach to the revision of a first draft, and the following check-list of questions for you to ask yourself may provide a practical basis:

(a) Have I got a clear focus on the heart of the topic or is some of my material irrelevant?

(b) Is the structure of my report clear? Do the arguments follow logically? Have I provided solid evidence for my views?

(c) Have I seen the wider significance of the topic, outside the particular cases studied? Have I analysed the significance of these cases or have I merely described them?

(d) Have I given the greatest weight to the most important aspects of the topic?

(e) Have I made full acknowledgement of my sources and given full references?

6. Check back over the script to ensure simplicity of style. It can be helpful to ask yourself if every word in your first draft is really necessary. Where you have used a long word, could you find a shorter one? Should you break up some sentences into shorter ones? Could you find simpler forms of expression, using active rather than passive verbs and concrete rather than more abstract terms: for example, 'They built no houses for five years', rather than 'The cessation of house-building operated over a period of five years'? Try to avoid pedantry: for example, 'a large number of people are coming' is perfectly correct, even though the noun 'number' is singular.

One of the most serious problems tutors have to guard against is that students are often tempted to base their reports and essays on passages copied out of books and journals, so that in effect they have at no point had to wrestle with the job of putting their own views or feelings or experience into words, or communicate these effectively to other people. This is why we have set this section on the arts of communication in the context of students' reports on practical projects and first-hand experience.

Activity 5: Research and discussion Look up (a) one or two essays you have written in any course you have attended in tertiary education or in training for the ministry, and (b) one or two field work reports you have presented in such a course. Read them carefully and judge how far you in fact conformed to the criteria outlined in guideline 4.

79

PRAYER AND WORSHIP

An indispensable part of the 'practical work' in which future Church leaders engage is deepening and extending their experience, and their understanding, of prayer and congregational worship. Obviously our expectations and feelings about forms of worship derive very largely from our previous experience, which means from the Christian subculture we belong to. It is therefore very important, now that there is so much contact between different cultures and subcultures, that we should get some insight into other forms of worship. But simply to attend a variety of Church services is not enough. Adequate preparation and briefing are needed. Students should be encouraged not only to record the details of action and language in the service, but to develop sensitive appreciation of the congregation's responses and of their own responses as well. A very useful exercise for students, working in small groups in fresh localities and drawing in members of the congregation, is to design, and where possible to lead, short services for special occasions, and to follow up with some estimate of the congregation's responses. In fact the analysis and writing of prayer and liturgy have great potential for theological training. Many Churches have prayer collections and manuals which could be very useful to students. And since worship is a very personal and intimate matter, students should be encouraged to keep some sort of journal of their experiences of worship, and of those 'peak' experiences of wonder or ecstasy which from time to time burst into people's lives and often reinforce the impulse to worship.

The same goes for private prayer. The approach sketched out in chapter 9 could be used here, noting especially perhaps the significance of St Teresa's reference to the use of books. The danger in this sphere of work is that a tutor's approach may be too academic and theoretical, too verbal. At the heart of any development in prayer are those deep, intimate searchings for the transcendent reality of God, those explorations, often in darkness and uncertainty, of the *meaning* of human experience, especially the meaning of love and suffering. As Hans Küng has written:

> ... In Jesus's suffering and death has there not been revealed by the incomprehensible God a definitive delivery from suffering which goes beyond all the incomprehensibility of God and which transforms suffering and death to life and to the fulfilment of longing? ... In itself suffering is mostly without meaning. When we look at the One sufferer a meaning is offered which ... has only to be trustfully accepted in order to know that God is present; however bleak, meaningless, desperate the situation may be. I *can* encounter Him, not only in light and joy, but also in darkness, sorrow, pain

and melancholy. . . . He is a God who lavishes His grace on those who do not deserve it . . . who does not demand love but gives it; who Himself is wholly love. In the light of Easter [the cross] was understood . . . as the deepest expression of His love. (70)

The deepest prayer often springs from the search for such profound insights. The sketch of an approach given on pp. 69–70 could be used in the present context. Perhaps the best way of giving prayer a practical basis is to make advice available to individual students from someone who is experienced in spiritual direction.

NOTES ON ACTIVITIES

Activity 1 I would expect you to make notes on roughly the following lines. In Example 15 the academic study would be connected with the influence of buildings on the people using them, and the planning of buildings to serve the main objectives of the users. In Example 16 the academic material would be the sociology of the neighbourhood, and the influence of existing social structures on the way the Churches do, and should, promote a deeper Christian living. In Example 17 the academic side may be concerned with the exercise of authority: how to exercise authority in a way which accords with Christian teaching and is in tune with the customs of the community concerned.

Activities 2 and 4 I would expect something on the lines I have sketched above.

Activity 3 Perhaps you were sent to a parish near your home, or a hospital or other institution, for a month's placement. If your experience was typical I would guess that you had hazy ideas of what academic topics you were supposed to find illustrated at that workplace, but had found the experience rewarding in getting to meet a variety of people and having the chance of observing in detail the working of an organization. You would be much vaguer over what personal or social development had taken place.

Activity 5 I would expect you to find that the formal essays you had written contained much more material quoted from books and journals than your field work reports, and that the reports had greater directness and bite than the essays. But I would also expect you to find that a number of long words in both could profitably have been replaced by shorter ones, and a number of sentences broken up into shorter ones also.

11

Self-assessment and tutorial comment

TESTS FOR SELF-ASSESSMENT

... when they give you back a mark, they don't seem to realize the individual impact that an essay can have—for example ... this can be the essay of the year that can make a break for you, after this your confidence goes. ... Of course the tutor isn't all that well connected with you, he doesn't know this is going on. To him it's just another essay and you're just another student, so you try and keep emotions out of it, you don't start crying in front of him or anything. The impact of one essay can be staggering on the person. *A student, quoted in* (68)

As we have noted, most formal examinations place their chief emphasis on memorized information and the comprehension of a specific subject discipline, i.e. the students' achievement under Objectives 1 and 2. However, there are cogent arguments for including a much wider range of objectives in the training of Church leaders. In extension and distance-learning courses therefore, tutors need to be very clear as to where they wish the real emphasis to lie, and how to balance the claims of the various objectives.

The *TEF Study Guides* present students with three sets of questions within the text. The first are mainly concerned with achievement under Objectives 1 and 2. The second set is composed of studies of concepts: an important element under Objectives 1 and 2. These two series, which are accompanied by answers at the end of each book, provide excellent tests by which students can assess their own progress in connection with those first two objectives.

Students cannot so easily assess themselves on the remaining objectives, but they need to make an attempt. Tutors may, for example, from time to time prompt them to ask themselves how near they think they have really got to the heart of an argument, or grasped the central theme and made it part of their mental furniture (subsidiary objectives (a) and (b), pp. 15–16, and Objectives 6 and 8). Or they may be encouraged to try to assess their capacity for handling professional relationships.

TESTS FOR TUTORIAL COMMENT

The third series of questions supplied in the *TEF Study Guides* under the heading 'Research (or Application) and discussion' are usually designed to promote progress under Objectives 4 (communication skills), 5 (application in new situations), 6 (analysing an argument), 7 (invention), 8 (assessing quality) and 9 (existential understanding and practical judgement). In the TEE context the answers to these need to be sent to the tutor for comment and marking, and the nature of that comment, as well as the marks given, will exert great influence on the students' attitudes, their confidence in their ability to study with success, and especially their gradual development of the more advanced skills.

Activity 1: Research and discussion Select a set of 'Research (or Application) and discussion' questions from a *TEF Study Guide*. Note down which Objective or Objectives you think each one is designed to serve.

THE ART OF TUTORING: STUDENTS' WRITTEN WORK

Some practical points are worth noting. It makes a lot of difference to students if tutors can handle their written work quickly and return it with the minimum of delay; this shows the tutors' real concern for the students and means that the material is still reasonably fresh in their minds. 'Rapid feedback promotes sound learning.'

The appearance of the student's script after the tutor has worked on it is also important. Students often feel very discouraged if their work is returned to them covered in scratchings and comments, particularly if these are not easy to read. It is probably most helpful if tutors restrict entries on the script to remarks about handwriting, grammar and spelling, and type their comments on treatment of the subject-matter on a separate sheet.

As regards the latter, the most helpful practice is to comment first on the strong points, the areas where a student has presented a good argument or shown initiative in finding relevant material. Adverse criticisms tend to be self-defeating. Weaknesses should be treated with care: only one or two should be taken up, at any rate in the early stages of a course; others should be left for later occasions. The comments should indicate how the students can overcome their weaknesses, and in relation to both strong and weak points should refer again to the Objectives, so that students can check their own development over the full range of competencies and skills. Sometimes additional sources of information or guidance can be suggested.

Activity 2: Stop, think and note Cast your mind back to the days when you were yourself studying and submitting essays and reports to your tutors for comment. Was your written work always returned promptly? What were your feelings when there was a long delay? How useful were your tutors' comments? How far were you conscious that your tutors were training you to assess evidence more carefully, to analyse arguments more precisely, as under Objectives 4–9?

In face-to-face conversation tutors can convey their appreciation of their students' strengths, and their concern to help them in overcoming weaknesses, by the tone of voice used and their facial expression. In distance learning, on the other hand, tutors have to ensure that the style of their written comment still conveys that flavour of personal interest. This aspect of support and encouragement is especially important when face-to-face contacts between tutors and students, and between one student and another, are infrequent.

AWARDING MARKS

The awarding of marks or grades is most helpful to students when some explanation is given of the standards or criteria applied in making the award. The list suggested in Rating Scale 1 may be useful; it can of course be modified for use with any particular group of students. Tick the left-hand box if the statement on the left is true; tick the second box from the left if the statement on the left is true to some extent. Similarly for the right-hand boxes.

Rating Scale 1: Essays and Reports

Structure					
Essay relevant to topic					Essay has little relevance
Topic covered in depth					Superficial treatment of topic

Balanced judgement emerges in essay					No balanced judgement emerges in essay
Argument					
Evidence accurately presented					Evidence inaccurate or questionable
Argument developed logically					Essay rambles, lacks continuity
Original, creative thinking					Little evidence of originality
Style					
Fluent writing					Clumsily written
Concise writing					Repetitive, verbose
Presentation					
Legible, well set out					Untidy, hard to read
Reasonable length					Too short/long
Sources					
Sources clearly acknowledged					Sources not acknowledged
References fully stated					References not stated
Mechanics					
Sentences grammatical					Some sentences not grammatical
Correct spelling throughout					Much incorrect spelling
Effective use of tables and figures					Tables, etc. add little to argument
Correct use of units, quantities					Some units incorrect

This rating scale is included here rather than in chapter 18 because of its direct relevance to distance-learning tutorial work.

Activity 3: Research and discussion Try out this rating scale on two or three of your students' essays or reports.

NOTE ON ACTIVITIES

Activity 2 I would expect your report to contain such comments as the following: 'There was often a long delay in getting my script back. Sometimes this made me angry; in the end it made me rather cynical. The commentaries were usually very brief and gave little guidance on my progress in relation to the higher order skills.'

On the other hand, you may have been lucky with some of your teachers and thus able to report that they took a lot of trouble to understand what you were getting at, raised questions about your non-academic experience, and suggested possible sources of additional material relevant to your interests.

12

Group Tutorials

STUDENTS' COMMENTS ON GROUP DISCUSSIONS

The following are comments on group discussions; 1–5 are by students, no. 6 by a tutor.

1. ... I'm afraid it was one of those silent tutorials. Again I don't know who is to blame—the eight round the table or the tutor. He will say something like, 'Well, what do you think of this?' and you look at the floor and you look at the wall, you look anywhere except at him. *C. M. L. Miller and M. Parlett* (71)

2. ... It just stops. Half way through the seminar it just stops.

Nobody speaks for two minutes. [What happens then?] Very little. The seminar leader breaks the silence. These silences are rather draughty at times. The seminar leader can't stand silence. He is always the one who breaks it. *J. Rudduck* (37)

3. ... Some lecturers come in and they just start, you know, like another lecture in the seminar. (37)

4. ... Well, I think part of the trouble is that we are just not prepared beforehand. *M. L. J. Abercrombie and P. M. Terry* (74)

5. ... The prime means by which you have got to communicate is by talking, and when you get out into the big wide world, if you can't communicate to someone else what your feelings are on a subject, you may as well give up. You have got to be able to talk. *P. Sheldrake and S. Berry* (75)

6. ... How do you handle the person who talks all the time? (37)

These quotations illustrate some of the problems of discussion sessions or 'seminars', a term originally used of a session introduced by a student reading a short paper prepared in advance. In universities and colleges discussion sessions are usually meant to uncover difficulties and misunderstandings which students have experienced in their academic work, whether in private reading or in attending lectures. As the comments quoted above indicate, students are not very enthusiastic about this approach. Sometimes they are shy of looking foolish; often they are unsure what the source of a difficulty is. In this chapter we look at a different and more active approach.

THE ART OF TUTORING: STUDENTS IN SMALL GROUPS

There are two points here on which tutors may wish to focus their efforts. In the first place the phrase 'group tutorials' suggests an emphasis on *tutorial guidance*, on attention to the problems, personal as well as academic, which students encounter in the course of their reading. This is of course a different aspect of tutoring from that described in relation to students' written work (pp. 83 84). At a first meeting tutors will probably wish to establish a personal quality in their relations with the group, and in students' relations with one another. Quite a lot of time can usefully be given to describing the tutor's own background, as well as getting individual students to describe theirs and say what they hope to gain from the course. An effective way of promoting this is to divide the group into twos or threes and ask members of each sub-group to describe their backgrounds and aspirations to one another. On re-convening the class as a whole, time can be given to bringing out the most typical and the most surprising features.

However, success in establishing the desired climate of relationships will depend on one vital factor: the tutor's own attitude. Some elements are especially important. One is a certain 'openness', a willingness to acknowledge that tutors do not 'know all the answers', that the course itself is not necessarily ideal for all comers, and that students do run into problems from time to time; that is, a willingness to be 'genuine' or 'authentic', to be one's 'real self', in one's relations with the class.

Another element is a genuine respect for the views of the students, a willingness to listen carefully to what any student says and make sure one has understood it correctly. This means appreciating the distinctiveness of people's individual responses and feelings, and recognizing the strength of their reactions to success or failure.

Tutors whose approach to their students is marked by these attitudes should have no difficulty in establishing that most important feature of a class: an atmosphere of trust.

Activity 1: Research and discussion How would you rate yourself on your readiness to accept students for what they are rather than for what they 'ought' to be?

High	Low

How would you rate yourself on your readiness to be natural or 'authentic' with students?

High	Low

However, tutors are only human, and not everyone will be able to maintain such ideals as these. In any case the shape and limitations of the tutorial role vary greatly from culture to culture, and indeed from college to college. And if group meetings are relatively infrequent tutors will naturally wish to re-establish this climate of relations at each session.

One of the first jobs tutors need to undertake is to discuss the list of educational purposes or process-based objectives presented to the students. Exercises 1–5 from ch. 7 will already have been carried out, and it may be convenient to break up the class into twos and threes again for reviewing them. There may also be queries on the content of the course.

ACADEMIC DISCUSSIONS: ASSOCIATIVE GROUP DISCUSSION

Secondly, on the intellectual side, tutors will wish to focus on developing the students' capacities for critical thinking (Objectives 6 and 8), for effective interchange with others (Objective 4), for independence of thinking (Objective 3), and for reflection on personal experience (Objectives 9 and 11).

Activity 2: Stop, think and note Remind yourself of an occasion when you have been a member of a discussion group. How many members were there? What took up most time—the lecturer talking?—two or three students who talked too much?—a general discussion in which all took part? How far do you consider that the tutor was trying to develop your critical thinking?—or your skills in speaking and listening?

To promote such qualities of thinking, some teachers in tertiary institutions have evolved a discussion strategy in which they encourage student-to-student interaction, and adopt a less dominant role themselves. This may be done in various ways. One of these techniques, known as Associative Group Discussion (AGD), takes the following form.

The first part of a session, perhaps 20 minutes in a 90-minute period, is allocated to a short task. To illustrate: the students are given a brief passage to analyse individually; or they read a short scene from a play, taking parts; or they inspect a slide or chart, or watch a short videotape; or role-play an incident; or read a report of a student project or field study. The tutor then asks one or more questions of a probing or controversial nature. The students do not know how the tutor or their fellow students have responded to the material offered, and there is therefore at once a basis of exploration and debate: an entirely different situation from a discussion session which follows up a lecture or a set book.

Activity 3: Research and discussion Devise an introductory task for an AGD session in a subject with which you are familiar. How would you ensure that it led into some critical thinking?

The situation is different in other respects also. Tutors who are determined to generate student-to-student exchanges, and to intervene only to steer the debate towards critical assessment of evidence and concepts, are likely to find two major obstacles: their own ingrained habit of making authoritative pronouncements, and the students' ingrained habit of depending on the tutor's authority as instructor. Both tutor and students have to learn new roles, and this process may be impeded by the climate of opinion and relationships in the institution, which profoundly influences the assumptions and expectations with which tutors and students approach their work. Tutors will, however, find it very helpful in cultivating their skills for such work, to record their discussion sessions on tape.

Activity 4: Research and discussion If you have access to a tape-recorder, arrange to record a discussion session. Count the numbers of contributions of the various members and comment on the quality of your own contributions. Were you clear/vague? concise/long-winded? appreciative/critical?

DISCUSSION SESSIONS IN LARGER GROUPS

Certain practical problems recur from time to time. In a class of more than ten or twelve students there are always likely to be some who are silent, or nearly silent. This may be because they prefer to absorb what others are saying; more often they are shy, or inarticulate, or too slow in response to be able to intervene. A tutor needs to be aware of all the individuals and—when appropriate—to invite comments from the quiet ones.

Some, on the other hand, are likely to be over-talkative or over-assertive, and these need to be curbed. It may be enough to say, 'You have made several very useful contributions which we all appreciate, but let us now see what other members of the group think.' If this does not have the desired effect it may be necessary to find time for a talk with them, and probe a little into the motives for their behaviour, having previously perhaps looked into the sources of one's own attitude to them. An alternative is to find jobs for them to do, such as acting as recorder for the group, which will take up some of their energy and offer some recognition of their enterprise.

Students who persistently make critical or hostile comments on others' contributions are more difficult to cope with. One needs to address them with courtesy and take their remarks seriously. Giving them a job may help; but some expert counselling may be needed.

Activity 5: Stop, think and note What experience have you had of over-talkative and/or over-critical members of a discussion group? How did the tutor deal with them? If not very successfully, what better ways do you think could have been used?

There may also be open disagreements: these can be a valuable point of entry into the area of subjective assumptions, a way of gently exploring perceptions and unvoiced value-assumptions which underlie the opponents' conflicting views.

Another aspect of students' participation in discussion is the precision with which they express their own views or understand the views of other members. Tutors can gradually promote more careful listening and more exact expression of ideas by tentatively re-stating a contribution: 'Are you suggesting that ...?' or 'I wonder if the last speaker did mean exactly what you suppose?'

ACADEMIC DISCUSSIONS: USING SUB-GROUPS

Alternatively, the class may be divided into groups of four or five members and presented with a short task to carry out, or a question to discuss, in a relatively limited time, followed by a brief period for an oral report leading into general discussion. For example, St Paul in 1 Corinthians 12, is in effect saying, 'Some members are claiming that they have the important gifts and are despising those who do not have the same gifts; what we as Christians should recognize is that we all need each other.' The tutor shows the class the photograph in *TEF Study Guide 17* (42), p. 161, of fishermen in the Solomon Islands, who need one another when they load their heavy nets into the canoe before setting out for the evening's catch, and then asks them a question, 'What are some of the ways in which the members of *your* congregation need one another?' This will induce the students to extend St Paul's message to a different setting. The task may even be extended further, to include such a question as, 'Is there any point at which you think such mutual dependence is overdone?' No more than five minutes may be needed on one of these questions to generate a debate; general discussion by the class as a whole is set going by the engagement of the students in the sub-groups first.

Or again, *before* opening up the idea of the mutual self-commitment of a man and a woman in marriage, the class might be shown the photograph in *Study Guide 17*, p. 80, of a Land Dayak couple in Sarawak, who no longer live in a traditional village 'longhouse' but have built a small house of their own. The sub-groups could take up the question, 'Do you think this will help them to commit themselves to each other more fully?' Thus in effect the sub-group approach would be used not only as a generator of discussion but as an advance organizer. That is, it will set the students thinking about some of the issues *before* these are taken up systematically in the next stage of the course (see pp. 55–56).

Activity 6: Research and discussion Devise two short tasks or questions, in a subject with which you are familiar, which could be used by a sub-group, (a) as a way of launching a general discussion on a recently studied topic, and (b) as an advance organizer. Describe how the two schemes you offer would operate.

ACADEMIC DISCUSSIONS: REFLECTION ON INNER EXPERIENCE

The accent in the above account is on the development of students' critical thinking, on their learning to articulate their opinions clearly, and on acquiring some independence of judgement. At some stage tutors will wish to open up discussion on the subjective aspects of personal experience emphasized in chapter 6. The change of direction from developing critical judgement to reflection on subjective experience will call for a conscious effort, but this aspect should not be left out of the picture. We discuss it in greater detail in chapters 16 and 17.

13
Memorization

If students have formal examinations to pass they will inevitably need to memorize certain basic information, and even if they have no examination ahead, they will in professional practice feel the need to have a great deal of factual information at their finger-tips. This chapter therefore is concerned with techiques for memorizing facts and figures.

PREPARING FOR A FORMAL EXAMINATION
•

Students preparing for a formal examination will need to have a sound knowledge of the facts and figures concerning the historical and literary background to the Bible and the history and growth of the Church, and also to be in full command of the arguments for and against particular doctrines and the views held by prominent theologians through the ages, as well as the range of evidence that supports new theories put forward in the light of modern knowledge. A practical way of preparing which tutors might recommend to their students is the following series of steps.

Example 19
1. Study some old examination papers and pick out those topics which seem to appear most frequently.

2. For each topic pick out all the notes you have made at different times on the subject, whether from lectures, sermons,books, journals, or tutorials, and sort them out into a logical order. Include any relevant personal experience. This procedure is similar to that for planning a report (see pp. 78–79).

3. Summarize the material for each topic in a logical order on a postcard.

4. Carry your postcard summaries with you and read them from time to time—perhaps when waiting for a bus or travelling by train.

Steps 2 and 3 call for some of the skills described in chapters 2–6: e.g. judging the relative importance of concepts and of evidence, Objectives 6 (analysing an argument) and 8 (assessing quality). They also demand 'deep processing' of the material you are summarizing, as described in chapter 3. Step 4 provides the spaced-out repetition which serves to imprint the material in the memory.

The rest of this chapter describes a variety of techiques. Some people find it easiest to memorize pictures, some to remember words, some neither in particular. So students need to choose those methods which best suit their own talents.

MEMORIZATION TECHNIQUES: SOME VISUAL SYSTEMS

Visual symbols can easily be demonstrated by rough drawings on a chalkboard, and students then be given exercises on them.

System A. Imagine a house or a human body and attach to each part one item of what you have to remember. For example, you wish to memorize the grouping of law codes in the Torah as listed by D. F. Hinson in *TEF Study Guide 10* (82), chapter 1:

Sketch a human body, and attach the first code—the Ten Commandments—to the trunk of the body, as the main basis for all human living. Attach the code of Deuteronomy to the two legs, as concerned with the concentration of worship in Jerusalem, an important development, and with the treatment of the poor and the unfortunate. Attach the Book of the Covenant to one arm, the Priestly Code to the other arm, and the Holiness Code, as the ultimate component of the Torah, to the head. Give yourself reasons for attaching particular items to particular parts of the body (or to particular rooms if you use a house instead), so as to fix them in your memory.

System B. Draw a map or chart which includes the information you want to remember, For example, you might make a chart to summarize St Paul's arguments in Galatians, distinguishing the following components:

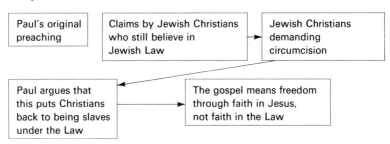

The process of sorting out these events into separate components in itself calls for the same sort of skills as preparing for a formal examination, above.

System C. Link numbers to pictures:
1 = anything tall and thin, e.g. candle, tower;
2 = anything shaped like a 2, e.g. snake, bird with long neck like swan or heron;
3 = object having three divisions, e.g. trident or three-pronged fork, fish-spear;
4 = object having four parts, e.g. window frame, picture frame;
5 = object having five parts. e.g. hand;
6 = object shaped like a 6, e.g. ladle;
7 = object shaped like a 7, e.g. signpost, flail;
8 = object with two circles, e.g. spectacles;
9 = object shaped like a 9, e.g. spoon;
0 = round object, e.g. sun, moon.

For example, the Exodus took place about 1200 BC. 1 and 2 are the *staff* which Moses threw down and the *snake* which it turned into; 0, 0 are the unleavened *cakes* the Israelites ate at the Passover.

MEMORIZATION TECHNIQUES: SOME VERBAL SCHEMES

Scheme A. Make up a rhyme which includes the required information; for example:
In fourteen hundred and ninety two
Columbus sailed the ocean blue.

Scheme B. Identify numbers with rhyming words:

1 = run,	4 = door,
2 = zoo,	5 = hive,
3 = tree,	6 = fix, etc.

Then make up an absurd or humorous sentence which includes the information, for example: 365 days in a year = There is a swarm of bees in that *tree*; I will *fix* up a *hive* for them.

Scheme C. Form a word out of the initial letters of a list of words. For example: education has five kinds of aims: Spiritual, Intellectual, Emotional, Social and Physical; arrange into order SPIES.

Scheme D. Impose an order on disconnected items. For example, a shopping list includes Bank, basket, shoes, pedals; write a story about them with something absurd or humorous in it; for example, 'I rode into town on my bicycle. One of the *pedals* came off and I fell off my bicycle. I was taking a pair of *shoes* for repair and they fell out of the *basket*. However, I fixed the pedal on again and eventually reached the *Bank*.'

Activity 1: Research and discussion Devise schemes for memorizing:
  (a) The three aspects of 'comprehension' set out under Objective 2 on pp. 7–8.
  (b) The nine Objectives listed in chapters 2–6 as Objectives 3–11.

Activity 2: Research and discussion Select some date or number which it is important for you to have at your finger-tips, and devise a scheme for memorizing it.

We may notice that some of these techniques are only useful in a literate society: e.g. the four steps suggested as preparation for a formal examination (p. 93) and visual system B. (p. 94). Others, however, could be used in a non-literate society.

All of them call for energetic thinking and the exercise of imaginative or inventive talent, as under Objective 7 (invention). The very business of thinking up new or humorous connections will help to lodge them in the memory.

14
The art of lecturing

COMMENTS ON LECTURES

... A lecture is a way of passing information from the notes of the lecturer to the notes of the student without lodging in the mind of either.

... You don't want to appear stupid: they ask, 'which part of it do you not understand?' and you don't have the nerve to say 'all of it'. *A student after a lecture* (83)

... Research shows that the recall of information presented in lectures is very poor: less than half is remembered immediately afterwards and half again is lost within a week. (79)

... Prof. X made several profound remarks to the jug of water standing on his table, with a humorous, twinkling aside to the pile of books on the table. *G. Highet* (84)

USING ILLUSTRATION

Lectures occupy eighty per cent or more of teaching time in many tertiary institutions; they are often the students' major source of information and stimulus to thought. Students—and not only students—often express discontent with the effectiveness of the lectures they attend, and the above quotations show how strong that discontent can be. Students have also specified their requirements: they want lectures to be 'clear, orderly statements, logically planned, emphasizing basic principles'.

In urban areas with mains electricity and access to audio-visual equipment visual material is now widely used to illustrate lectures. The use of slides and overhead projector (OHP) transparencies (and, where an episcope is available, pictures in books) not only adds authenticity, but enables tutors to make exact comparisons of distinctive features. Films can demonstrate clearly the procedures of a decision-making meeting or a Church service; and the showing of film has been simplified by the introduction of cassettes. However, films are expensive to produce and facilities for clear projection may be lacking. Video recording is tending to take over in many institutions, and with the development of battery-driven, hand-operated recorders these will probably spread fairly rapidly in developing countries, though the scarcity of servicing and repair facilities is likely to be a deterrent.

Such sophisticated teaching aids are not the only ones available. A great range of simple do-it-yourself techniques can be used where projection facilities or electric power are unavailable, or financial resources are slender. Many tutors devise their own posters and charts, or build up collections of large pictures. A simple flannelgraph can be made by stretching part of an old blanket tight over a frame, and mounting pictures or diagrams on pieces of rough material such as blanket, blotting paper or sandpaper. Simple models can be made from scrap materials and painted, and a sheet of hardboard coloured with a matt paint makes a perfectly adequate chalkboard.

However, the use of visual illustration does not of itself necessarily make for a good lecture. The lecturer has also to decide precisely what features of a picture or slide, or what sequences in a film or video recording, to pick out for attention. And even at a large formal lecture it can be more effective to ask questions which prompt the audience to say what *they* think are the implications of what they see before them. The examples given on p. 91 and the questions arising throughout chapter 10 illustrate what may be needed.

PREPARING A LOGICAL STRUCTURE

Even when attractively illustrated, however, lectures, as continuous talk from a speaker to an audience, often fail to communicate a clear understanding of the subject matter. The *structure* of a lecture, the shaping of the argument, is of crucial importance.

There are three main forms of 'structure' or 'shape'. The first, the 'classical' pattern, may be illustrated by chapter 1 in Harold Taylor's *Tend my sheep* TEF Study Guide 19 (41). An important general concept is stated at the beginning: the shepherd as a well known figure among agricultural peoples, with a note on how the idea was used by Old Testament and New Testament authors. A second section explains the various tasks performed by a shepherd, again with reference to biblical uses. A third explains various ways in which a shepherd may exploit his position and abuse his sheep. A fourth expounds the various ways in which Jesus offered a model for the 'Good Shepherd'. Each section is clearly distinguished from the others, and each section is itself developed in a clear logical order of points,

A second pattern of structure is problem-based. The lecturer opens by stating a problem, whether in the form of a controversial question or of some concrete case report, such as those quoted on pp. 32 and 52 above. Two or three alternative solutions are then presented, and probably compared. For example, after stating the problem of the meaning of St Paul's word 'justification', a lecturer might trace the various possible interpretations, with the arguments for and against them.

A third pattern is the 'sequential' structure: the sort of presentation needed for a historical account, for example of the sequence of events in one of St Paul's missionary journeys.

Not all good lectures conform to one of these patterns. What is chiefly important is a clear pattern of argument, a well marked and logical organization of the evidence, and clear conclusions. Every lecture should demonstrate the ways of thinking and uses of evidence which characterize the subject.

Activity 1: Research and discussion Search out your notes of lectures that you attended as a student, or the handouts outlining them, and decide which type of structure they exemplify. Sketch out the pattern of argument.

Activity 2: Research and discussion Sketch the patterns of three lectures you have given or might give in your own subject area, to illustrate the three main types of structure.

ENSURING CLEAR EXPLANATIONS

Equally important are the *explanations* of the concepts and argument the lecturer is trying to convey. There are three main types of explanation. 'Interpretative' explanations clarify the essential meaning of some idea or issue, providing answers to such questions as 'What is ministry?'. 'Descriptive' explanations give an account of a process or a procedure, answering such questions as 'How were the definitive versions of the books of the Bible arrived at?'. 'Reason-giving' explanations offer answers to such questions as 'Why did King Herod have John the Baptist beheaded?', or 'Why is it so important to read the Bible regularly?'. Lecturers need to make sure that the explanations they give are absolutely clear.

Activity 3: Research and discussion Get together with two or three colleagues and devise one question for each of the three types of explanation listed above. Arrange for each person to work out their own explanation for each question and then take four minutes (no more) to give that explanation to the others. If you have access to a tape-recorder the exercise will be doubly useful; but even without a tape-recording each of you can learn a great deal from the comments of your colleagues on the clarity, direct-ness and intelligibility of each of your three explanations.

At their first attempt to carry out Activity 3 people will probably show hesitations, unfinished sentences, more than one 'um' or 'er', and vague phrases like 'you know'. A good way to get rid of these distractions is to take time for a little practice in formulating explanations: picking out the most important points in what is to be described; putting these central points into very simple language, using everyday words, sketching out the steps of the explanation to an imagined audience, and summarizing the argument in the simplest possible terms. And needless to say, when actually giving a lecture one needs to be clearly heard, which means speaking loudly enough to carry to the back. This is best achieved by keeping one's eyes on the people in the back row, as if one was speaking directly to them.

GETTING STUDENTS INVOLVED

So far we have been concerned with the logical order and clarity of a lecture. In many institutions lectures are devoted almost exclusively to conveying the basic information and structure of a subject, the essential concepts and evidence. There are, however, many techniques which will engage students more fully and actively with the lecturer's intentions, and enable them to gain a sharper grasp and appreciation of the arguments put forward. In that process they may become involved again with the critical thinking and the relating of book-learning to first-hand experience which they need.

One such method is to provide 'signposts', some of which will indicate the place of an individual lecture within the course as a whole, while others mark out the structure of the lecture itself. For the former one can easily prepare a note outlining the shape of the whole course, showing which recommended books relate to which lectures, and including comments on the themes to be taken up. For each individual lecture one can highlight the crucial steps in the argument, whether by numbering them 1, 1.1, 1.2; 2, 2.1, 2.2 etc.; by drawing an evolving diagram of the topic on the chalkboard; or progressively revealing the steps by uncovering them on a previously prepared chart. Often the simplest method is to distribute a handout giving a skeleton of the lecture—an outline showing the logic of the argument, not a full exposition. This also saves students the hassle and distraction of racing to get notes on paper. Handouts are especially useful when diagrams or statistical tables are needed.

Activity 4: Research and discussion Work out a series of 'signposts' for the lecture outlines you sketched in Activity 2.

An alternative—as noted above—is to present the lecture material in the form of a real-life problem, from which an 'academic' problem, a matter for investigation, can be drawn and the stages in moving towards two or three possible solutions signposted.

Activity 5: Research and discussion Look at the problem-based lecture outline you sketched in Activity 2, and re-state it in the form of a real-life report, giving rise to an academic problem, with the possible solutions.

Another way of presenting a lecture effectively is to break into it with a practical exercise. At the simplest level, when some of the audience start dozing off, one can simply stop and tell them to stand up, turn round, and sit down again. The mere interruption and physical movement will give them—and the lecturer—a fresh start. A useful technique during a particularly complex or difficult part of a lecture is to form 'buzz groups', that is, ask students who happen to be sitting next to one another to form groups of three. Then pose a specific question about the difficult passage, and allow, say, five minutes for students to work out their responses. This will not only break the strain of a difficult exposition, but provide an immediate check on whether one's explanation has been successful. Buzz groups are also a useful way to challenge students to check a fresh idea against their own experience.

> **Activity 6: Research and discussion** Devise a scheme for the use of buzz groups in the lecture outlines you have already drawn up.

A more elaborate way of providing student practice and getting feedback at the same time is the 'pyramid' technique. Ask individuals to spend (literally) two minutes considering a specific question—for example, 'What information do we need for solving the problem posted on the chalkboard?' Then ask them to form pairs and spend five minutes on the further question, 'What method *could* be used for handling this problem?' Finally, get adjacent pairs to form fours and consider the question, 'Which of these methods would be best for this problem?', allowing ten minutes for this part. The reporting back will not take long, and will not only bring out students' difficulties clearly, but also reinforce the lecturer's explanations.

This technique can also be used to train students in the skills of writing, note-taking etc., by using photocopies of essays for discussion of their quality and of the criteria for judging them.

> **Activity 7: Research and discussion** Devise a scheme for using pyramid groups in the lecture outlines you have already drawn up.

The temporary use of small groups in this way can help to vary the pace and liveliness of a lecture. Other types of brief practical 'interruption' might be a three-minute scripted role-play, or the reading of a scene from some well-known drama.

Various other techniques can be used for making the content of lectures more accessible to students. Lectures can be recorded on cassette and kept in the library for students to refer to, or a file of handouts can be built up for reference. One can reserve five minutes at the end of a lecture for students to raise questions or check on their notes; or invite them to form pairs and check together on their grasp of the material and report back; or suggest they make carbon copies of their notes and hand them in for checking; or offer an 'instant' questionnaire of, say, five questions on the lecture content, for them to answer by writing 1 for 'yes', 2 for 'not sure' and 3 for 'no', and hand in at once.

> **Activity 8: Research and discussion** Devise a conclusion for each of the lecture outlines you have already drawn up, using one or other of the above ideas.

(To illustrate one of the techniques described in chapter 14, side 1 of the cassette mentioned on p. 2 shows how a topic which occurs in almost every theological syllabus, that of the Synoptic Problem, may be handled in a set of lectures. The cassette may be purchased from Gerald Collier, 4 Robson Terrace, Shincliffe, Durham DH1 2NL, UK, for the equivalent of £3 post paid.)

15
Syndicates and other small-group methods

VARIETIES OF SMALL-GROUP TECHNIQUE

As a preliminary to this chapter, look again at the students' responses to work in small groups quoted on p. 86, 87.

We have already discussed several different uses of small groups: in the context of Group Tutorials, lecture techniques and practical field studies. Small groups can also work very profitably on library-based assignments. These are all useful and legitimate styles of group work. However, tutorial teams who believe in the over-riding importance of our Objectives 4–11 may find it worth while to experiment with a syndicate-based approach.

PUTTING SYNDICATE METHODS INTO PRACTICE

In this type of organization a class of, say, twenty-five students is divided into 'syndicates' of perhaps five students, and the bulk of the work consists of a series of assignments carried out by these syndicates working as small teams. For much of the time this will be in the absence of a tutor, who will be circulating among the groups. This pattern may be followed for the whole of a course designed to follow a published syllabus, or—perhaps wisely if on a trial basis—for a particular project. The syndicates hand in written reports to the tutor at the conclusion of each assignment, and these form the basis of a plenary session in which the tutor summarizes them and consolidates the conceptual structure as it emerges. This pattern has three distinctive features: (a) the small-group work is at the centre of the academic study; (b) the assignments draw on a variety of selected sources as well as on the students' first-hand experience; and (c) the student-led syndicate work alternates with tutor-led plenary sessions. The heart of the technique is the intensive debate within the syndicates, which, as shown by quotations 4 and 6 on p. 27, should not inhibit individuals from developing their own distinctive opinions.

When this technique is working well it shows two striking advantages. In the first place there is an increased involvement of the students in their academic studies, a stronger motivation, which is revealed in various ways. There is better attendance at timetabled sessions, and the homework required for discussions is done more conscientiously. Students are willing to spend a lot more time and energy on the work, and they search more actively for information outside the prescribed sources.

Secondly, students will increasingly be practising the higher order skills: expressing their ideas cogently (Objective 4); applying what they have learned to new settings (Objective 5); analysing an argument (Objective 6); devising new schemes (Objective 7); and assessing the quality of an argument (Objective 8). These skills show themselves in various ways. Students are noticeably more critical in their approach to their reading. They look for, and gain, a stronger sense of the personal meaning of the subject matter for them; and a richer appreciation of the variety of opinion and experience involved in the study of any complex problem. They become more keenly aware of the provisional nature of current knowledge in their subject and less concerned to be told the 'correct answers'. They also make progress under Objectives 9 (existential understanding and practical judgement) and 10 (team work skills). As we shall see later, syndicate methods also offer excellent scope under Objective 11 (getting inside cultural assumptions).

Activity 1: Research and discussion Cast your mind back to any occasion when you worked for a substantial time in a group of four or five people, collaborating closely in carrying out a job. Check over the features listed in the above two paragraphs to see how far they match your experience and how far they do not. If your group did not work very effectively, what explanation, if any, can you offer?

However, syndicate-based courses do not by any means always work well. The technique poses problems similar to those of Associative Group Discussion (see pp. 89–91).

PRACTICAL PROBLEMS WITH SYNDICATE METHODS

With AGD the basis for realistic and profitable discussion is the short practical exercise provided at the start of a session. But in syndicate work the groundwork of the discussion derives from the search for information, evidence and interpretations which enable a syndicate to formulate a response to the questions posed. Different members of a syndicate will usually have been searching different sources and drawing on varied first-hand experiences. Seeking out a sufficient range of resource material at a suitable academic level calls for a big investment of time by the tutor, and so does the preparation of tasks or questions for the assignments. These are likely to seize the attention of the students more readily if they are based on problems arising from their own experience (see pp. 55, 56).

In discussing AGD we noted the change of role demanded of both teachers and students, and the same is true of syndicate work. Because for most of the time the syndicates are working on their own, the tutor cannot give them uninterrupted attention as an instructor or 'authority'. But the tutor's influence is still very great, and can operate in several different ways. Tutors may automatically step into the role of an 'authority' who delivers what 'ought' to be thought. They may act in collusion with a group to mask awkward differences of view, or 'generously' answer all the queries students ask and so kill the real debate in a group. Sometimes, too, tutors describe their new role as more emotionally and intellectually demanding than the traditional one, and report feelings of inadequacy and lack of academic and social competence. And some have difficulty in making the reverse shift of role when they re-assemble syndicates for a plenary session to consolidate the material studied, i.e. to ensure adequate attention to Objectives 1 (basic knowledge) and 2 (comprehension of subject discipline).

The institutional context also has a critical influence. In colleges where senior staff are tied to a traditional kind of formal examination system, tutors may have difficulty in establishing syndicate work.

Activity 2: Research and discussion Look back into the school/college/university where you have been a teacher. What would you say was the outlook of the senior staff on methods of teaching and examining? Do you think that any particular institution would or would not have been favourable to syndicate-based work? Where would the major influence have lain in such a case?

For students too, a very big adjustment of outlook is necessary for syndicate work—much more than in AGD. Students are apt to feel that they are lost in a strange district without a map. They have to be advised that the 'rules of the game' are now different: they are no longer required to assimilate knowledge from their tutors, but have to build up their own knowledge, drawing on the available sources. At first many will be unable to grasp what this means, or will be sceptical about its reality. Tutors will need to give patient guidance, for example in distributing resource material or jobs within a syndicate, or in arranging for the drafting of reports. Special attention to the students' perceptions of the demands of their examinations, and their perceptions of the proper functioning of a syndicate will be needed. If students expect to be assessed by an examination which tests mainly memorized subject matter, they may be unwilling to invest time or commitment in the open explorations that characterize a syndicate-based course, and will tend to adopt the 'surface' approach (see pp. 13–15).

It is generally desirable to form syndicates on a self-selection basis, as students will choose as fellow members those with whom they expect to be able to work happily and effectively. However, in some cases it may be advisable for the tutor to take some part in arranging membership, to avoid personality clashes or get a better balance of talent.

Activity 3: Research and discussion Assemble a group of three or four students and ask what they think their examiners in previous stages of their education have required as top priority; and what they think the examiners will be looking for at the end of their present course. How far are they correct? Should those priorities be different?

A comparison between the AGD and syndicate techniques as applied systematically in a complete course can be illuminating. Both aim to promote the skills of critical thinking. In AGD, however, the discussion sessions run parallel to other, probably lecture-based, methods of teaching and study, whereas in a syndicate-based course the whole subject content is embraced in the course. This accentuates the importance of the assessment methods, which must reflect, and be known to reflect, the students' involvement in the exploration of problems and evidence, and must give due weight to the higher order skills. A clear distinction between assessment of the achievement of a syndicate as a working team and assessment of individual students' improved skills and understanding is also essential. We discuss this point more fully in chapters 18 and 19.

When the system is operating with reasonable success, students show a noticeably more open and critical approach to study, and a greater depth or vitality of learning; they are able to break free to some extent from the compulsion to memorize masses of information, while still remaining aware of the need for precision.

A final comment on the technique. We have looked at one form of syndicate-based organization, which incorporates all the central features. However, this is not the only pattern. The size of the syndicates may be larger; the tasks and source materials may be differently organized; and methods of reporting back and consolidating the work done may be different. But for any tutorial team wishing to experiment with syndicate-based work the pattern outlined here is recommended. References to other experience are given in the section on Further Reading.

THE OVERALL IMPACT OF SMALL-GROUP METHODS

To the many uses of small-group techniques described in earlier chapters we have now added syndicate methods. At this point we may usefully follow up the discussions in chapter 4 by considering the overall contribution of this type of work to students' development.

Given a suitable climate of opinion, and a clear awareness on the tutor's part as to the potential of small-group work, we may expect students to show several lines of development. They are likely to be far more aware of the way relationships evolve in a group of people, and of the way they themselves function in that context—of their impact on others and others' impact on them. They are likely to have discovered to what extent they have skills in leadership or management. These are not results which can be in any way guaranteed. Tutors cannot *change* people by these methods, but they can establish conditions, create situations and ask questions, which may set students moving, and wishing to move, in certain directions. Students will only be stimulated to practise and develop these skills if they are working towards goals on which they set a high value. If tutors attempt, whether on purpose or by the spontaneous impact of their personality, to *train* students in these respects they may find the effect is to increase students' dependence while they are present, and that the influence tends to disappear in their absence.

Activity 4: Research and discussion 'Qualities like initiative ... ability to work with others ... will only be displayed by individuals, and therefore practised and developed, if the individuals are working towards goals they value.' Can you quote any experience to support or to refute this view? In what ways have the methods advocated in this book made, or failed to make, provision for this principle?

NOTES ON ACTIVITIES

Activities 1 and 4 I would guess that you would record some such experience, perhaps in a voluntary club at a college or Church, and that you would confirm the points about heightened motivation; but that you have had very little experience of this kind in academic study and cannot therefore endorse any of the points about critical thinking. One point that might emerge is the disruptive effect on a syndicate of a personality clash within its membership.

Activity 2 I would guess that you would be able to identify one institution of either kind, and that you would attribute the main influence to one or two very senior members of staff, such as the Principal and a long-standing head of department.

Activity 3 I would expect your students to report that previous examiners appeared to be concerned almost exclusively with correct information, correct knowledge of accepted views, and correct use of basic techniques. I would also guess that there would be some uncertainty or ambivalence about the priorities that might govern the thinking of the examiners of their present course, and that you would to some extent share these hesitations.

(*To demonstrate some of the techniques described in chapter 15, side 2 of the cassette mentioned on p. 2 is devoted to the use of small-group techniques, particularly syndicate methods, for the organization of work on the Synoptic Problem. Details of assignments are given in the leaflet which accompanies the cassette. The cassette may be purchased from Gerald Collier, 4 Robson Terrace, Shincliffe, Durham DH1 2NL, UK, for the equivalent of £3 post paid.*)

16
Exploring other cultures

SOME CHRISTIAN RESPONSES TO THE DIVERSITY OF CULTURES

... Medieval (Christian) thought saw divine purpose manifest everywhere in the world of nature. ... The real world disclosed by the work of science (on the other hand) was one governed not by purpose but by natural laws of cause and effect. ... There is no place for miracles or divine intervention ... as categories of explanation. ... Within this world-view it is (only) possible to keep a place for religion as a deeply inward and private experience. ... The Bible, on the other hand, is dominated by the figure of the living God who acts, speaks, calls, and expects an answer. *Lesslie Newbigin* (23)

... More recent times have seen much closer contact between Christians and those of other faiths and ideologies. In the cross-fertilization of ideas and attitudes which has followed, it has become plain that dialogue does not ask either side to 'give up' its position. Yet in the exploration between deeply committed women and men come those occasions of mutual recognition when honesty has to admit that they are in the presence of the God who has been discerned in varied ways by different peoples, but whose ways with us are one. ... the Word of God is not confined to the church of Christ, but the Holy Spirit is active everywhere. The resonances of the Word are to be heard throughout the whole of creation, and across the wide spectrum of faith. *John Poulton* (89)

... In the early phases of Western expansion the Churches were allies of the colonial process. They spread under the protection of the colonial powers: they benefited from the expansion of empire. In return they rendered special service to Western imperialism by legitimizing it and accustoming their new adherents to accept compensatory expectations of an eternal reward for terrestrial misfortunes, including colonial exploitation. *A group of African theologians* (90)

... The important question to ask about a myth or a story is not about its 'literal "factual" truth' but about the underlying vision of reality reflected in it. ... Is this consistent with the values of the Kingdom of God? The Church can bring together people from different communities, different cultures, who can share their experiences, pool their myths or stories, learn to hear their inner meaning. *Charles Elliott* (24)

... The soul comes to the mystery of the darkness in which it loses all sense of the love of God, all understanding of where it is or where it is going. It thinks it is getting lost. Indeed it is getting lost to what it knew and tasted, and going by a way in which it neither tastes nor knows. To reach a new and unknown land and travel unknown roads, a man cannot be guided by his own knowledge. He must rely on nothing of what he understands, tastes, feels or imagines. *St John of the Cross* (91)

In chapter 6 we looked at some of the sources of conflict between members of different cultures. We noted particularly how misunderstanding can arise from differences in *perceptions* and in *value-assumptions*. Individuals may see the same situation in quite different ways; they may hold different values, or different priorities among their values. In this chapter we look at ways in which people training to be Church leaders may learn to understand these subjective forces in members of other cultures, and in themselves. In achieving this understanding they are in a far stronger position to build a stable relationship of mutual respect with members of a different culture, based on those features and characteristics which they do evidently share with them.

USING CASE STUDIES

In very many countries today the differences of culture between different groups of people are likely to be conspicuous. Thus the tutor's problems lie, first, in assembling suitable material for study, such as case studies or reports, and second, in resolving how students can most effectively learn to probe into the implications of that material, as regarding both the characteristic assumptions of the contrasted cultures and the students' own personal responses. These are subtle and elusive matters to discuss, and if a principal aim at this stage is to enable students to appreciate the depth and power of the half-conscious forces in themselves and other people, then tutors will find themselves dealing with very sensitive areas of their personalities. A syndicate pattern of organization is therefore advisable, so that students can dig down into their own feelings and express them to their fellow students without any real or imagined approval or disapproval from a tutor. The formulation of those responses can then become a group matter, rather than a personal statement in the face of a tutor's possibly uncomprehending judgement. The following example, based on a passage from A. C. Krass, *Go ... and make disciples* TEF Study Guide 9 (29), shows how a case study might be handled.

Example 20

A strong pagan chief ruled the M—— tribe by means of force, inspiring fear in all his subjects, whom he kept in constant warfare with surrounding tribes. His will was law, and he and those in authority under him were held in awe—one might almost say they were worshipped—by all his subjects.

A Christian mission was set up on the other side of the river from the chief's village. The chief hoped for personal gain from the N—— missionaries' presence, and so at first he was favourable to their being there. After a time it became clear to him that the missionaries were undermining his authority by, for example, giving shelter to those who fled from his punishment. He tried to force the missionaries out, but the missionaries called on the newly-established colonial government to defend them. This was the first time that the chief had experienced the force of colonial power, and he learned that it was something to be feared.

When the people saw how the chief was powerless, his authority over them weakened. More and more of them moved across the river and settled in the Christian village which the missionaries established. They sent their children to school, they farmed by new methods, and one by one they were all baptized and became members of the Church.

The missionaries and those who were in authority under them were held in awe by all the people. They developed a code of regulations for the village, and all who violated any law were disciplined.

Now what actually happened here? On the surface, it may seem that a tremendous transfer of allegiance took place. But when we look closer and ask what the people's allegiance was both before and after their conversion, we see that their conversion represented simply a transfer from absolute, unquestioning allegiance to the chief and his lieutenants, to absolute, unquestioning allegiance to the missionaries and their helpers. The M—— Christians did not become free, and they did not become mature and adult. They remained children, or slaves, but in another man's house. There was struggle, but it was not between the old nature of the people themselves and their new nature, it was between the old ruler and the new. Those who were ruled remained the same.

Here we could pose such questions as: How did the converts see the authority of the missionaries? (–as absolute and unquestionable). How did they see the Church? (–as an authority alternative to their Chief's; no indication of the Church as an agency of a loving God). What value assumptions were indicated? (–that they must vigorously obey the authority of the Chief or the Church). How far would you say that the M—— Christians saw themselves as loved by God? What evidence is there? What evidence would you expect to find if, at some later stage, they began to 'know themselves as those who have been enslaved' ((26) p. 6)? Or, beyond that, to 'see that whatever bound them before need not bind them any longer' ((26) p. 6)? Have there been any marked differences of opinion among the members of your group about the interpretation of Dr Krass's report? If so, how far can you explain these in terms of differences in people's perceptions of the M—— tribe? How far in terms of differences in the priorities among people's own values?

Activity 1: Stop, think and note How far would *you* say that the M—— Christians saw themselves as loved by God? What evidence is there? What evidence would you expect to find if, at some later stage, they began to 'know themselves as those who have been enslaved'? Or to 'see that whatever bound them before need not bind them any longer'?

USING ROLE PLAYING

An account of this technique was given in chapter 10, where the examples given were intended to clarify pastoral or counselling methods for a Church leader in a rural congregation. They could equally be used for the purposes of this chapter by substituting such questions as: How does the teenage rebel see his situation in relation to his father?—in relation to other teenagers?—in relation to the Church? How does the father see these situations? What are the priorities among the father's values? It could well emerge that *both* set a high value on family closeness and family loyalty, as well as on reasonable freedom of action for the teenager and reasonable adherence to certain parental regulations; but that the orders of priorities among the shared values are very different.

Beyond this area of debate are the questions that probe into the students' own responses: Were there any sharp differences of view in the group? Can these be traced to sources in the students' individual personalities?—to different perceptions of the teenage rebel's situation?—to different emphases or priorities among their values?—to differences between the cultures to which different individuals among them belong?

Activity 2: Research and discussion Write a script for a short role-play exercise on a conflict between a parent and a teenage son or daughter. Explain how the parent and the child see the situation, and how their values differ.

DEEPER EXPLORATION USING DRAMA

The trial scene from Bernard Shaw's play *Saint Joan*, already quoted (pp. 36–38) as presenting a conflict typical of certain sub-cultures, could also be used to raise such questions as the following.

Example 21

1. How did Joan see the authority of the Church in relation to her worship?—to her voices?—to her wearing of men's clothes? How did she justify her views?

2. How did the Church authorities see Joan's insistence on wearing men's clothes?—on regarding her voices as giving direct commandments from God?

3. What evidence is there that Joan genuinely believed in 'obedience'? What were her priorities as to where she owed obedience?

4. Would you regard Joan as having 'integrity'? If your answer is 'yes', draft a definition of integrity that would suit Joan's case. If your answer is 'no', give some explanation for your view. (To answer this question you may find it helpful to read the rest of the trial scene, and perhaps the rest of the play.)

5. What motive do you think lay behind the Church authorities' insistence that Joan should accept the Church's view about Joan's voices?

6. How do *your* Church authorities regard the obedience of its members?—to the Church authorities themselves?—to their community's traditions?—to members' individual consciences?—to an inner commandment from God?

Activity 3: Research and discussion Where do *your own* sympathies lie? Do you find yourself supporting Joan or the Church authorities? Can you suggest any explanation of how you came to support one side or the other? Have you yourself experienced this kind of conflict, between your individual conscience and a religious authority?

DEEPER EXPLORATION USING A NOVEL

Example 22
The novel chosen for study here, *The River Between*, by Ngugi Wa Thiong'o (92), is the story of a young African, Waiyaki, who belonged to a tribe inhabiting two ridges, Mameno and Makuyu, with the river Honia flowing between. Waiyaki was rather exceptional, as a boy and as a man, easily attracting trust and loyalty. His father, of equally distinctive character, took him as a boy to a sacred grove Kerinyaga, and taught him that the white men, who were gradually taking over their country, could not be fought with physical weapons but only by a leader who learned all their wisdom and all their secrets. The people of the tribe would one day cry out for a saviour; and he implied that Waiyaki might be that man. So he sent him to Siriana, the white men's settlement where the missionaries taught people about Christianity and had a school. Waiyaki attended the school for several years. Two leading young men of the tribe, Joshua and Kabonyi, became Christians, and Joshua set up a Church in Makuyu, with Kabonyi as his assistant. Joshua was rather like an Old Testament prophet, denouncing all the customs of the tribe that were prohibited by Christianity, such as polygamy and female circumcision. Joshua had two daughters, the younger of whom, Muthoni, rebelled and joined the circumcision ceremony, saying: 'It is beautiful to be initiated into womanhood and learn all the ways of the tribe.' But the wound became infected and she died. The elders of the tribe said Christianity had contaminated the hills and their tribal god was angry; Joshua's followers said the girl must have had an evil spirit and nothing but evil could come of the old customs.

At this time the policy of the Mission was tightened and only the children of Christian parents were admitted to the school. Waiyaki, by now a mature young man and a competent scholar, remembered his father's words, and called insistently for the tribe to start its own schools. His call was soon accepted with enthusiasm. Schools were set up which were 'symbols of the people's thirst for the white men's secret magic and power', and Waiyaki became a popular headmaster: 'the pride of the hills and the pride of Kameno', known everywhere as 'the Teacher'. Meanwhile Kabonyi had left Joshua and reverted to the tribal customs. He was old enough to be Waiyaki's father, and he deeply resented Waiyaki's popularity.

But as time went on, Waiyaki found himself always 'hungry for something that would take possession of the whole of himself'. He felt 'those regions of the heart where doubts and fears struggled in the darkness'. He was dedicated to the development of the schools, but he more and more felt an urge to bring about a reconciliation between the Christians and the non-Christians, between Joshua's followers and Kabonyi's followers. But Kabonyi now set up a movement known as a Kiama, with the aim of getting all the non-Christians to take a binding oath of allegiance to the purity of the tribe. At the first big Kiama meeting the opinion went entirely in favour of Waiyaki, and Kabonyi felt publicly humiliated. But then Waiyaki chanced to meet Joshua's second daughter, Nyambura. Both of them were in some sense searching for an unknown ideal, both yearning for reconciliation between the two sides, and they fell in love. To Joshua this seemed a betrayal by Nyambura of her father and her Christianity, since Waiyaki was not a Christian. To Kabonyi it seemed a betrayal by Waiyaki of the oath of allegiance to the purity of the tribe, since Nyambura was an uncircumcised Christian.

Here we reach the last chapter, which opens with a big assembly of the tribe called by Kabonyi and the Kiama.

Even Waiyaki was affected by that great hush that fell over the land. He could hear his heart beat and he told himself: I must not fear. And he stood at a raised piece of ground and looked at the people; at their expectant faces and eyes. *Salvation shall come from the hills.* And he saw that many people had come and had filled up the initiation ground and the slopes of the hills. Some had climbed up trees. *A man shall rise and save the people in their hour of need.* And he remembered his father. Waiyaki realized all too suddenly that this was the hour, the great hour of need. The tribe needed him now. Nyambura needed him now. And he needed himself too. Kabonyi was a destructive element. He did not know the way. But Waiyaki was ready, there to move together with the people, to grope in the dark maybe, but together, searching for the light, looking for the way.

He began to speak. At first he made a small speech; thanked the people for coming; asked them to bear with him. He had been stunned by the recent development in the hills: hatred and rivalry such as would destroy the people. He outlined his struggles in the service of the people, especially in the now ending year; it was the year that saw the transformation of the hills. He told them of his attempts to get more teachers. He had succeeded although it was a difficult task. But when he came back he was accused by the Kiama of being a traitor. Some people, he said, had gone out at night and were singing that he was a traitor. Let those people now stand in front and accuse him publicly. If he had wronged the ridges, people would know what to do with him.

A big roar of 'The Teacher' greeted his brief speech. Some cried 'The Teacher is right,' though they did not know what he was right about. Others cried 'Let Kabonyi come forward.' And Kabonyi stood up with dignity. Their unfinished battle was now on.

He was once a Joshua follower. Now he was the Leader of the Kiama and he lived in Makuyu. He spoke with the authority of a man who knows the secret workings, evil and good, in men's hearts and in the country. His big accusation was that Waiyaki was unclean. He had *thahu* and if he continued teaching the people there would be darkness instead of light. When a girl called Muthoni died because she was visited by evil spirits, Waiyaki had taken her to the white man's hospital in Siriana, and was never cleansed. As he was a leader, his *thahu* had visited the tribe. It was now for the tribe to take action. For Waiyaki was a greater menace than the people realized. He was in league with the white 'man, who had brought a secret religion to quieten the people while the land was being grabbed by their brothers.

He sat down. Waiyaki noted that Kabonyi had carefully avoided any mention of Joshua or Nyambura. Why? He thought that he too would avoid dragging in the name of Nyambura but he would speak of unity. Now, or he would never get another chance.

Kabonyi's speech had been greeted first with stony silence and then with murmuring. The sun was slowly going down.

Waiyaki's voice was calm and compelling. His eyes shone and anger began to stir in him, for now he knew without any doubt that Kabonyi was determined to see his ruin.

'What does Kabonyi want?' he asked. 'Who first followed the white man and embraced the new faith? Who betrayed the tribe when Makuyu and Kameno and the other ridges could have risen in arms against the white man? We are all children of Mumbi and we must fight together in one political movement, or else we perish and the white man will always be on our back. Can a house divided against itself stand?'

'No-o-o,' they roared in unison.

'Then we must stand together. We must end the ancient rivalry.'

People seemed moved, and when he sat down they rose and, as if of one voice, shouted: 'The Teacher! The Teacher!' And when Kabonyi stood to speak, people began to press towards Kabonyi as if animated with the desire to tear him into pieces. And they would have done it and that might have been the end of threats to their teacher, but for Waiyaki, who stopped the crowd. 'No! No!' he shouted. 'Do not touch him.' It was as if Waiyaki at that moment realized that Kabonyi and the Kiama were also in their way an expression of something felt and desired by the tribe.

They listened to their Teacher, their saviour, as if they would say, We shall never give you up. As for Waiyaki, he was amazed because he did not know that he had such power over the people.

He could not even listen to what Kabonyi was saying about the break with the missions, and about purity. It was only when Kabonyi mentioned something about the oath that Waiyaki grew attentive. And he found that every other person was attentive to Kabonyi, who now spoke with a broken voice, full of grief. To break oath was one of the most serious crimes that a man could commit. Such a person was doomed to destruction.

People knew that Waiyaki had taken an oath given by Kiama never to contaminate the tribe with impurity and never to reveal the secrets of the Kiama, secrets which involved the political destiny of the hills. So when Kabonyi said that Waiyaki had broken that oath people roared back 'No-o-o.' How could they believe it? How could they believe that Waiyaki was in league with Joshua for the destruction of the ridges? They again shouted 'No-o-o!' Waiyaki remembered Nyambura at home and he felt afraid. He wanted to go back to his hut and see if she was safe. He felt relieved and heard Kabonyi's next words.

'I can prove to you, beyond any doubts, that he is a Joshua's man in spite of his oath.'

They cried 'Prove! Prove!' He waited for the confusion to die and then said, 'He is marrying his daughter.' Another hush fell over the land before there were cries of 'No! Not the Teacher,' and Waiyaki trembled slightly and he waited fearing, yet did not know what he feared. He wanted to rise and speak to the people and tell them about Nyambura and how he had gone to rescue her, but his knees failed him as he saw Nyambura in the gathering twilight, brought by Kamau and two other young men. She was made to stand before the people.

'Let him deny her.' Kabonyi threw the challenge. And the people shouted 'The oath! The oath!' as if they were warning their Teacher. Waiyaki stood up and his eyes met those of Nyambura. And he remembered her on this very ground that time she was praying alone; it was the day he first held her in his arms. And she looked beautiful now. She looked like a lamb on the altar of sacrifice. And Waiyaki knew that he could not deny her now, that he could not go back on his love for her.

There was a long silence. People held their breath. One woman screamed 'The oath!' and the cry was taken over by the other people.

Waiyaki tried to silence them but they would not listen. They only cried 'The oath' and their cry was echoed in the forest. And how could he tell them now that he had not betrayed them, but this was not what he meant by unity; that he was not in league with Joshua? How could he tell them that he meant to serve the hills; that he meant to led them into a political movement that would shake the whole country, that would tell the white man 'Go!'

An elder stood up. Waiyaki could not hear what he was saying for his mind was full of many thoughts and doubts that came and went. Waiyaki and Nyambura would be placed in the hands of the Kiama, who would judge them and decide what to do. It was the best thing and the crowd roared back 'Yes' as if the burden of judging their Teacher were removed from them. They went away quickly, glad that he was hidden by the darkness. For they did not want to look at the Teacher and they did not want to read their guilt in one another's faces. Neither did they want to speak to one another, for they knew full well what they had done to Waiyaki and yet they did not want to know.

This narrative could be used to raise such questions as the following:

1. How did the general members of the tribe see Waiyaki after his first speech?—after his second speech?—after Kabonyi's first speech?—after Kabonyi's second speech?

2. How did Waiyaki see his love for Nyambura in relation to his loyalty to the tribe?—in relation to his position as a highly respected teacher?

3. How did Joshua's followers see the customs of the tribe, such as female circumcision? How did they see the gradual infiltration of the white men?—the authority of the Kiama?—Joshua's authority?—God's love for themselves?

4. How did Kabonyi's followers see the customs of the tribe?—the

gradual infiltration of the white men?—the authority of the Kiama?—the devotion of Joshua's followers to Christianity?

5. We can see indications, in Waiyaki and Kabonyi, of a commitment to such values as loyalty to the tribe, adherence to an oath, loyalty to a loved person, self-advancement, revenge for humiliation, building up the education of the people, respect for the elders of the tribe, reconciliation of the two factions, expulsion of the white men. What do you think was the order of priorities given to these values by each of the two men? Give the evidence for your view.

6. St Augustine referred to some people he knew who were not Christians as having a 'naturally Christian soul'. How do you think he would have judged Waiyaki? Give your evidence.

7. What do you think of the Siriana missionaries' policy in relation to such customs of the tribe as female circumcision?

8. What differences of opinion have there been in your group? How far can you explain these in terms of differences in your perceptions of this tribe? How far in terms of differences in the priorities among your values?

Activity 4: Research and discussion Draft your own answer to Question 5 above.

NOTES ON ACTIVITIES

Activity 1 I would expect you to say something about the sense of unquestioned authority which the members of the M—— tribe attached to their Chief and to the Church. The evidence for this is that the missionaries were held in awe by all the people—as the Chief had been before; the people remained children or slaves, did not become mature or adult. If at a later stage they began to shake off this dictatorial authority, they might be expected to show a more relaxed, and perhaps more critical, attitude to authority.

Activity 2 I would expect to read some discussion of the parent's looking for respect and obedience from the child, and perhaps referring to the time and energy and money that had been spent on the child, while the latter feels aware of 'growing up' and demands to be treated in a more grown-up way—not ordered about, given more freedom of action. But these views might be far from the normal expectation in some societies. Probably both parent and child share a belief in a good social order, in family harmony, in general conformity with the community in which they live. Tutors using this material with a student class might find a clash arising. If so, it could be useful to make some effort to trace the sources of the clash; but this will call for some care and tact in raising questions.

Activity 3 I would expect to find the majority of readers in some cultures identifying more closely with St Joan; those in other cultures with the Church authorities.

Activity 4 I would expect to see something on the following lines. Waiyaki is deeply committed to several of the values described in the question: loyalty to the tribe, adherence to an oath, loyalty to a loved person, building up the tribe's education, respect for the elders, and reconciliation between the two factions. But I would expect there to be considerable divergence of view in a group, about the order of precedence. For Kabonyi I would expect to find at the top of the list loyalty to the tribe, then adherence to an oath, respect for the elders, self-advancement, and revenge for humiliation. The evidence would be presented in a series of excerpts from the chapter quoted, or from the summary.

17

Gaining Self-knowledge

We cannot draw a sharp dividing line between the methods for promoting an understanding of another culture and those for promoting self-knowledge. Both depend, if they are to have any existential value, on our providing materials, or creating situations, which elicit a real engagement on the part of ourselves and our students. In this way we can jointly build some insight into the dominant assumptions of our own culture, of ourselves, or of another culture. In chapter 16 the questions posed on the Examples were focused on the characteristic features of other cultures. In this chapter we look at ways of directing our attention towards self-knowledge. The examples presented in these two chapters are interchangeable for classwork.

SHARING SIGNIFICANT EXPERIENCES

One way of approaching the quest for self-knowledge—developed at the University of the South, Sewanee, Tennessee, USA—is to invite a member of the class or group to describe an incident which was personally significant, marking perhaps a turning point in life, or a fresh insight into the Christian faith, and which aroused deep feeling. The individual is asked to give enough detail to enable the rest of the group to enter into the experience and in some degree share the emotions and thoughts of the occasion; perhaps even to share the belief that God was speaking through that incident.

Alternatively it could be some internal crisis or conflict which constitutes the 'incident', rather than an external event. Apart from anything else, reporting and clarifying the experience is a valuable exercise for the person concerned, expressing subjective feelings not previously put into words.

In either case the tutor then asks if the group can suggest some metaphor or simile which will in some sense 'crystallize' and give extra meaning to the incident or experience. The Bible is full of metaphors: Jesus speaks of His disciples being 'as wise as serpents and harmless as doves'; there is 'the eye of the needle', 'the mustard seed', 'the sower'. And everyday life is full of analogies: In English we talk about being 'over the moon', 'slipping on banana skins', 'sticking out like a sore thumb'. In other cultures and languages people might think of sayings like 'selling the skin before you've killed the beast', or 'slowly slowly builds the fire': every culture has its equivalents. These 'metaphors' serve to generalize an incident without making an intellectual analysis or abstract statement about it. They may relate to the world of people's everyday activity, or to the culture of the community they belong to, or to their religion or ideology: the structure of beliefs and convictions they hold—in the Christian tradition to the Bible, the liturgy, the writings of the saints. This approach makes no attempt to probe into the value assumptions implied in the experiences reported; it is essentially an exploration of the way situations are seen and felt and suddenly change, an exploration of perceptions.

Activity 1: Stop, think and note Look into your memory and recall some incident in your life which had this kind of significance for you, and sketch out an account of it on the lines indicated.

LITERATURE, DRAMA, ART, MUSIC

Another approach to the exploration of the subjective world is through the study of works of imagination which present the big issues of life. Great works such as Shakespeare's plays, Mozart's operas, Tolstoy's novels or the great paintings of the Italian Renaissance are the traditional areas of engagement for members of Western cultures and many members of other cultures also. For numerous individual Christians they provide unrivalled opportunities for eliciting deeply-felt responses touching the profoundest issues of life. But we have to recognize that many people find such works difficult to enjoy. For whatever reason, whether of language, musical idiom, or contrasting culture, they cannot respond at any depth. Tutors therefore need to turn to whatever works of imagination will have a validity for the community with which they are concerned. There is a wealth of material from which selection can be made: in India perhaps the epic *Mahabharata*, or in Chinese-speaking areas the delicate *Eighteen songs of a nomad flute*; many developing countries have a growing fund of modern indigenous literature, such as Ngugi's novel quoted in chapter 16; and in societies without a literary tradition there are myths, legends and folk-tales that can be used.

At a more popular level, too, the romances, thrillers and adventure stories of paperback and magazine fiction can and often do arouse deep feelings (just as pop music and jazz can fire the emotions), which spark off wide-ranging argument on questions of right and wrong that are directly related to the cultural background portrayed. And the mass media of radio almost everywhere, as well as widespread cinema and television, offer a similar opportunity of choice, whether through serious programmes on universal themes such as the Japanese film *Harp of Burma*, or through the so-called 'soaps' and situation dramas, which frequently touch on deeply-felt social and ethical issues of the day.

USING A FILM

A story told by a film or TV programme has an immediacy of impact not shared by purely literary media, because it is conveyed by a mixture of verbal and non-verbal modes of communication like those of everyday experience. Personalities and relationships come across through a richer and more complex texture of words, gestures, tones of voice and facial expressions than in a novel or printed play. Thus a well-chosen film can be used to open up significant issues and prompt students to reveal themselves to themselves.

The following example shows the use of a fictional film well known in many countries: Lumet's *Twelve Angry Men*, a study of the jury at a murder trial.

Example 23

At the start of the film the members of the jury are convinced that the accused man is guilty. But one member feels that they should at least re-examine the evidence, and begins to sow doubts in their minds which eventually lead to a reversal of their first verdict. The film is a character-study of a person of unusual integrity, who is able to raise awkward questions about the evidence and sustain his own uneasy doubts in the face of opposition and boredom. This character, Davis, is played by the well known American actor, Henry Fonda.

The first assignment for students reads as follows:

1. In the story presented by this film the jury at first reach the tentative conclusion that the accused is guilty; afterwards they regard this conclusion as mistaken. How do you account for the process by which the character taken by Henry Fonda, Davis, influences the others to reconsider their first decision?

(a) What traits of personality do you see in him that contributed? On what evidence do you base your view?

(b) By what steps of procedure did he move?

(c) How far did he condemn those with whom he did not agree? Quote incidents.

(d) In what respect (if any) could he be said to have 'forced' or 'coerced' other members of the jury?

(e) Did the gradual change of view impress you as true to your knowledge of people? Explain why.

2. Davis is thought by many viewers to be a man of unusual integrity.

(a) How does one arrive at such a judgement about a person? Think of a friend or acquaintance who in your opinion has this quality: what sort of *evidence* have you based your judgement on?

(b) What evidence is provided in the film that could lead a viewer to consider Davis to be a man of integrity?

(c) On the basis of this film, formulate a definition of the quality of 'integrity'.

Some of these questions are designed to bring out students' interpretations of motives and relationships, some lead them to voice their subjective perceptions of the situation studied, and some oblige them to sharpen their understanding of a value concept—that of integrity. At later stages in the debate it could be useful to refer to works of literature bearing on this central concept, such as the two already exemplified: Shaw's *Saint Joan* and Ngugi's *The River Between*, or T. S. Eliot's *Murder in the Cathedral*. Some questions can be designed to bring out the different scales of priorities the students hold among their own values. Others can bring out the contrast often to be seen between people's conscious attachment to a moral principle and their actual behaviour. Tutors may also wish to prompt a discussion about the nature of moral argument, of moral reasoning, and its relationship to Christian moral teaching. Fictional programmes on radio and TV can be used in a similar way.

The classroom organization of the work will vary from tutor to tutor. For this sort of assignment a small-group approach can have certain advantages. In a small self-selected group students are more likely to tolerate the inevitable differences of responses and views, arising from differences both of culture and of temperament and personality, which emerge and have to be worked through. An important aspect of the work is to enable students to appreciate the unexpected depth or shallowness of their own responses, as well as the variety and richness of other people's cultures, and of their own.

Explorations like these have much potential. One film or programme will open up dialogues between Christians of different outlooks and varying degrees of commitment, with some perhaps finding that they are less than wholehearted and echoing the man in the Gospel who said to Jesus: 'I believe; help my unbelief'. Another may be used to open up discussion on the moral basis of public life. So the students may appreciate the advantages of a non-dogmatic, non-ideological approach to political and economic problems, and see a new meaning in St Paul's words, already quoted, that in Christ 'there is neither Jew nor Greek, slave nor freeman, male nor female' (Gal. 3.28). Overall there is great potential here for promoting that ideal for which Jesus prayed: 'for those who believe in me . . . that they may all be one' (John 17. 20–21).

KEEPING A DIARY

Students also need the private probing of their own real motives and feelings. A very useful tool for this purpose is a diary or journal. When from time to time we try to record an experience, the very act of putting it into words on paper opens up unsuspected realities about our own character. We see more clearly into our ambitions and desires, our self-concern or our self-deception. As St Teresa wrote, 'Self-knowledge is so important that, even if you were raised right up to the heavens, I should like you never to relax your cultivation of it; so long as we are on this earth, nothing matters more to us than humility.' But the keeping of a notebook, whether to enrich self-knowledge or to deepen prayer, is a very sensitive part of a student's life, and its privacy must be respected. It may also help them to capture something of those other moments which we all treasure, sometimes referred to as 'peak' or 'transcendent' experiences, where time seems to stand still. They may arise in many ways: from music, from literature, from sexual fulfilment, from a glimpse of the divine, from a sunset sky.

IMPLICATIONS FOR TUTORS

Another technique for deepening students' self-knowledge is role-playing (see pp. 112, 113). However, when used for this purpose it can arouse disturbing feelings, and only an experienced tutor should undertake it. But there are no sharp dividing lines, and much self-discovery may emerge from a role-playing exercise directed to the understanding of, say, authority relationships, or of another culture (see chapters 10, 16).

How far tutors succeed in promoting their students' self-under-standing depends partly on the sort of questions they put to them; but it probably depends more on the tutors' own attitudes and the climate of relationships they establish. As already noted (p. 88), the critical factor in the delicate exploration of inner responses and unspoken assumptions is the openness of tutors about their own shortcomings and their evident concern to understand fully what students are trying to say or or to express.

All Christian tutors will presumably wish to see their students growing into a real honesty or integrity in getting to know themselves, and developing a real concern to recognize the evidence about their own characters. These are qualities which should transcend academic influences and regional cultures—and also human pride. But such qualities obviously cannot be taught by classroom instruction or private advice: they can only be elicited by people of similar outlook, in a climate of mutual respect and trust.

VALUES UNDERLYING THE POLICIES PRESENTED

Readers working their way through this book will probably realize by now that it is written from a particular standpoint, and based on rather strongly held values.

Activity 2: Stop, think and note Return to chapters 2–6. Looking at the relative amounts of space and emphasis given to the different aims or process-based objectives, what would you say was the order of priorities among the eleven Objectives listed? Quote your evidence. How far would you say that these priorities suit your institution? How far do they suit your personal outlook?

As author, my own scale of values necessarily reveals itself not only in the priorities or emphasis given to the eleven Objectives, but— especially—in the material selected for chapter 6 and this present chapter, and the questions suggested for use in the latter.

Activity 3: Stop, think and note Re-read the Examples in chapter 6 and this chapter on *Saint Joan, The River Between*, Tribe M——, and *Twelve Angry Men*. What priorities do you detect among the values implied by these Examples and the comments upon them, particularly with regard to the importance of the individual conscience?—to the relation between the individual conscience and the authorities of an institution such as the Church?—to the relation between an individual's conscience and the culture of that person's community?—to the relation between an individual's conscience and the evil which he sees at work both within and around him?

Activity 4: Stop, think and note Much space and emphasis has been given in this book to the active involvement of students with the subject matter being taught, with the tutors who are guiding them, and with their fellow students. Less emphasis is placed on the assimilation of instruction given by the tutors. How far does this balance of emphasis accord with the outlook of your own institution?—with the outlook of the communities from which your students come?—with your own personal outlook?

Activity 5: Research and discussion Look again at the striking passage by St John on the Cross quoted on p. 110. In the clashes of cultures and the turmoil of political and economic change there are surely many occasions when Christians engaged in education have great difficulty in seeing what they should be doing, where they should be going, and what their top priorities should be, if they are to follow God's will. Have you had any such experience? If so, what were the circumstances? How far were you able to sort out the confusion of aims and priorities? How far was the confusion an intellectual one, how far was it rooted in a sense of being abandoned by God? How far were you able to find effective support in your college (or other) community?

NOTE ON ACTIVITIES

Activity 5 It is difficult to speculate, but I would guess that some of the most acute problems experienced would revolve round the exercise of authority, whether in an institution or a community or a family. Such bafflement may be encountered at various levels. Perhaps the problem is simply one to be thought through, the various aspects being analysed and a solution worked out on the lines described in chapters 4 and 10; that is, it mainly calls for intellectual clarification and creative thinking. Secondly it may be a problem of conscience, of duty: what *ought* you to do? Which value, which obligation should be the over-riding one, the one that God would command? A third alternative takes us closer to St John of the Cross: the 'problem' may be felt as a total darkness in which none of the usual signposts mean anything, and one can only wait patiently in the hope that God will in His own time throw some illumination on the direction He is calling us to follow. At this point especially, one needs the support of a Christian community.

PART 5

ASSESSMENT IN RELATION TO SPECIFIED
OBJECTIVES

18

Assessment techniques for academic objectives

SOME REMARKS ABOUT EXAMINATIONS

... The idea [of an experimental paper] was that there would be a reward for genuine understanding of the scientific principles underlying the course. ... It should test things which cannot be swotted up [in] the last week. There is more reward for thinking ability. *A staff member* (71)

... We all refuse to recognize that we vary in our marking. We all know it doesn't work, but it's too difficult to do anything else. ... We all admit to ourselves that the degree mark is not very accurate and we ought to get down to discussing the criteria on which we mark. Then it becomes personal and subjective and painful to people. *A staff member* (71)

... Some students ... deliberately interacted with the system: they button-holed staff about the exam questions; sought them out over coffee; made a point of discovering who their oral examiner was, what his interests were, and, most of all, deliberately attempted to make a good impression on staff. This for them seemed to constitute a very large part of what the exams were all about. *A report* (71)

... Exams completely fill me with fear, especially these ones we are coming to—it's so dreadful it's not true. *A student* (71)

... In theological college there is a way of eating a boiled egg which reveals the progress made by the candidate in his spiritual life. *A cynical observer*

... I'm just going off to buy another goldfish. I tell all my neurotic friends to get one. Watching them go round and round, looking after them, it keeps you sane. *A student*

THE PURPOSES OF ASSESSMENT

The pattern of assessment has enormous influence on the direction and focus of students' effort, and is thus a powerful instrument in the hands of a teaching institution. As one educationist has put it, 'the spirit and style of student assessment define the *de facto* curriculum'— the programme of studies as it operates in practice. The problem in the present context is how to ensure that the assessment techniques used do in fact test, and are seen to test, the objectives that have been specified. As has been emphasized throughout this book, there is a whole range of very different aims to be achieved or attempted, so we clearly need to look very carefully at what we are trying to get from our assessment system.

First we have to recognize that in many colleges the examination system is used as an instrument of discipline, to ensure that students do a required amount of work, and conform closely enough to the standards of conduct set by the college to be permitted to sit the examination. A policy of this sort, however, being based on coercion, implies that much of the course is only studied under threat: with a heavy pressure on students to adopt a 'surface' mode of study, and a corresponding sacrifice of developments under Objectives 3–11.

We return, then, to the assessment of academic objectives (see chapter 2). Tutors will first be looking for feedback as to the effectiveness of the course—its suitability as a programme of study for their particular students, and as an organized system of teaching for their particular institution, given the objectives of its sponsoring bodies and its role in training, grading and recommending its students. They will also be looking to provide feedback to the students as to how far they have achieved those wide-ranging objectives.

A first requirement in designing a sound assessment system is to ensure that the testing technique really tests what it is meant to test. All too often examiners set questions which they hope will test students' powers of critical judgement, but which in practice largely test their knowledge of basic facts and accepted views. We need to ensure the *validity* of a particular testing technique: does it in fact measure achievement under the objective for which it was intended?

We need to check whether what students *think* they are being tested for matches what those who mark the tests are actually giving credit for.

Activity 1: Words Explain the meaning of the word 'validity' (in its examination context) by considering what is meant by measuring achievement under Objective 4 (communication skills).

We also need to check for *reliability*, that is, whether a given examination paper will yield the same marks when given to the same class by the same teacher on different occasions, or when marked by different examiners.

Another point to clarify is the *intention* of the examination. Are the marks or grades intended simply to represent the standards reached by a particular class of students at a given time, with most of them clustering round the average or 'norm', and small numbers gaining exceptionally high or low marks? Or is the examination designed to test students' *mastery* of certain knowledge or skills—as a car driver or a pharmacist has to reach a certain standard of performance which matches up to the safety of road users or the needs of patients seeking medicaments? In this case a student has to gain perhaps 80–90% of the marks in order to pass, and if the teaching has been sound the great majority *will* gain these high marks. The former type of examination is known as norm-referenced, the latter as criterion-referenced.

Following the logic of earlier chapters in this book we need to work out quite precisely the balance of emphasis to be given to each different Objective, and the techniques to be used. We also need to tell students just what we are, and what we are not, trying to assess in each phase of the assessment system. We shall therefore look at each of our eleven Objectives in turn, beginning, with the more specifically 'academic' ones: i.e. 1 (basic knowledge), 2 (comprehension of subject discipline), 5 (application in new situations), 6 (analysing an argument), 7 (invention) and 8 (assessing quality).

ASSESSING ACHIEVEMENT OF KNOWLEDGE-BASED OBJECTIVES

Objective 1 (Basic knowledge)
The simplest way to test students' knowledge of basic material over the full range of a subject is by means of 'objective' tests. These are termed 'objective' because, if suitably designed, there will be no

'subjective' element in judging the answers, no room for bias in the examiner, no doubts or ambiguities in marking them. They are of two kinds: 'short answer' questions, and 'selected answer' or Multiple Choice Question (MCQ) tests. The former are easily illustrated:

Example 24: Short answer questions
What three sorts of 'judgement' did St Paul refer to in 1 Corinthians 4? Which of them did he regard as the most important? *TEF Study Guide 17* (42)

By what word is 'demon' translated in another language known to you? What is the usual meaning of this word? *TEF Study Guide 17* (42)

What did the Hyksos kings and the Israelites have in common? Where did the Hyksos come from? When did they enter Egypt? What was the name of their capital city? For how long did they rule Egypt? *TEF Study Guide 7* (101)

MCQ tests too are easy to mark, but call for a lot of care and skill in their design. The following guidelines may be useful:

1. Usually *four or five choices should be offered.* To offer only three increases the likelihood of getting the correct answer by chance.

2. In designing a question it is important to *phrase the opening section clearly and simply*, and to ensure that all the answers offered have exactly the same construction. What this means is shown in the following example.

Example 25: A Multiple Choice Question
St Paul thought of 'justification' as:
(a) Finding a justification for one's actions
(b) Deriving from a belief in Jesus
(c) Forming a just view of God
(d) Deriving from good deeds
(e) Being a just and righteous person

Here the opening section is vague, and the answers offered for choice are of different constructions; we should rewrite as follows:
Which of the following meanings for the word 'justification' comes closest to St Paul's view?
(a) Finding a justification for one's actions
(b) Being in a good relationship with God through faith in Jesus
(c) Forming a just view of God
(d) Being in a good relationship with God through doing good actions
(e) Being a just and righteous person

Here we have avoided giving a clue to the correct answer by offering all the possible answers *in the same grammatical form* and *with similar types of wording*. We have not only *kept the opening simple in wording*, but have *avoided putting in unnecessary information*, as would be the case if we had said '. . . St Paul's view as expressed in the New Testament'.

3. We also need to make sure that *the answers are all unambiguous,*

that the wording of the question does not contain *phrases which hint at the correct answer*, and that *one answer is definitely the best* and the other four obviously less appropriate (not necessarily incorrect but less well matched to the question).

4. Even when we keep strictly to such principles, faults in the questions can easily be overlooked, so draft questions should always be *field tested*, even if only on a small scale among colleagues.

Activity 2: Research and discussion Design three MCQs, each offering four or five alternatives, on an area of your subject.

Objective 2 (Comprehension of subject discipline)
Here too we can design MCQ tests to assess achievement, but again skill and care are needed, and field testing is essential.

The example just given might in a more elementary course be regarded as a test of achievement under Objective 2 rather than Objective 1. Concepts which at an early stage in a course indicate some grasp of a subject discipline, may at a more advanced stage be regarded as basic knowledge.

Another technique for assessing a student's grasp of a subject is the 'structured question' or 'Modified Essay Question' (MEQ). For this type of test a suitably complex case study, factual or fictional, or a connected passage from a book, is presented, with a series of questions requiring perhaps 50 words each for the answer. For example, the case study quoted on pp. 111–112 (29) could provide the factual basis for such questions as

Example 26: Modified Essay Questions
(a) What evidence is given to support the view that the members of the M—— tribe had changed their everyday living?
(b) What evidence is given to support the view that the members of this tribe had not become mature Christians?
(c) What sense of 'freedom' do you think Dr Krass meant when he wrote 'The M—— Christians did not become free'?
(d) What kind of evidence would you look for, to check whether the M—— Christians had in fact begun to 'know themselves as having been enslaved'?

This pattern makes it possible to test quite specifically the students' use of evidence, their understanding of concepts, and their command of the characteristic types of argument *within the limits of the subject matter* so far studied. The questions do not call on memorized knowledge of historical facts or theological theories, nor demand the

131

organizing of a lengthy argument. And a series of six or eight questions can be made progressively more searching.

Activity 3: Research and discussion Select a case study or report from a book, and design a set of six to eight questions which will test the students' grasp of the nature and logic of the subject discipline.

Activity 4: Words Explain the meaning of the word 'reliability' as applied to examination techniques, by considering the use of the above techniques for assessing attainment under Objectives 1 and 2.

TESTING CRITICAL JUDGEMENT AND HIGHER-ORDER SKILLS

Objectives 5 (Application in new situations), 6 (Analysing an argument), 7 (Invention) and 8 (Assessing quality)
To test the development of these powers we need to set tasks that require their exercise, and preferably avoid any appearance of testing achievement under Objectives 1 and 2.

One technique is to make individual or group projects the basis on which students must prepare individual or group reports or dissertations. Each phase of the student's work is marked: (a) analysing the problem to be tackled; (b) surveying resources needed; (c) planning the work entailed; (d) carrying out the plan; (e) reporting results; (f) a critique of the whole exercise. The practical problem for tutors may be finding or inventing suitable projects rather than actually marking them. The assessment schedule below is designed for a fairly elaborate exercise, with several sub-groups working on different schemes, and the final stage a conference where each small small group presents a formal report of its findings. It could easily be adapted for less ambitious class exercises. Individual projects could be assessed as suggested on pp. 79, 85.

Section A: Preparatory stages (a)–(c)
Thoroughness of background reading
Initiative in searching out fresh sources
Contributions to discussion and response to others' ideas
Ability and willingness to communicate
Planning and management of group activity
Skill as chairman or secretary of group

Ability to comprehend ideas
Practical ability in dealing with human situations
Judgement in seeing flaws in arguments
Originality, creative flair, problem-solving ability
Others

Section B: Written report (d)–(e)
Clarity of expression, precision
Ability to select relevant information and present it suitably
Quality of diagrams
Use of references
Conclusions; critical review of achievement
Group mark for cohesion and editing
Others

Section C: Plenary conference (e)–(f)
Selection of material for conference
Organization and planning
Initiative and enthusiasm
Clear explanation and reporting
Use of visual illustration
Answering questions
Others

A second technique is a more complex form of the MEQ type of examination, based on a factual case study or research report; or alternatively on a 'simulation', or carefully composed fictional case study of an organization or community. (In the near future such case studies and simulations will be available in appropriate subjects on computer programs.) The questions can be designed specifically requiring students to analyse the structure of an argument (Objective 5), work out novel solutions to a problem offered (Objectives 5 and 7), assess the validity of a complex argument (Objective 8), or extract the core of the argument from an 'unseen' passage (Objective 6), according to the occasion. Tests of these kinds can also be built into a distance-learning package for subsequent tutorial assessment and comment. The following example, based on a passage from Charles Elliott's *Praying the Kingdom* (24), illustrates this technique.

Example 27
... the whole biblical record can be read as God's longing to transform his people by the power of his love. He accepts us as we are, caught up in personal and structural sin as we may be, and offers us a quality of relationship that enables us to transcend the power of that sin in our own lives, and to engage spiritually and politically in the struggle to make ready for the coming of the Kingdom.

Critical readers will say that this account of the classical doctrine of atonement makes sense, if at all, only at the level of the individual's own spiritual development. It thus falls under the condemnation, it may be argued, of a privatized religion—which we have already condemned as a pathological reaction to the man-trap.

A reply consists of two arguments. First, remember the 'marriage' of my individual drives on the one hand and the socio-economic institutions and processes which they support on the other. On this account, a universal assault on those drives is an assault on the institutions and processes which exploit and damage the poor and the vulnerable. 'Structural sin' may well be identifiable as an entity, a force for evil, apart from the sinfulness of any one individual.

In the ultimate, however, with many time-lags and untidinesses, institutions and structural relationships do respond, slowly, hesitantly, with the grace and speed of a hippopotamus with bloat, to the collective moral ethos. Change that and, in the very long term, you will change the world. Slavery, child labour and the cruder forms of racial discrimination are examples.

Second, the doctrine of atonement is essentially dynamic. By its very nature, it releases a new energy into the spiritual environment. *Because* I am, amazingly, accepted, forgiven, I am more than ever determined that what was wrong, is wrong, will be put right. For reasons that we will come to soon enough, that will not catapult me into the kind of hyperactivism we have already discounted. It will, however, mean that I am not only more aware of my social impact; nor only that I am more critical of it; the 'new life' I am made capable of appropriating by degrees will be lived out *both* in the interior world of meditation and private prayer, *and* in the woof and web of my structural relationships. Precisely because I am set free of the guilt, the existential anxiety of my responsibility for the suffering of the world, I have greater energy, greater freedom, even greater joy to confront and confound the inequities and injustices of which I am part. It is in this sense that guilt, properly dealt with by acknowledgement and forgiveness, becomes a source of transforming energy.

Let us finally turn to the lower jaw of the man trap—powerlessness. How can that be made into a positive charge in our prayer life? Perhaps the answer is already obvious. For it is central. It is when we acknowledge ourselves as power*less*—as caught, trapped, unable to achieve any improvement in either our own inner lives or in the external forces to which they give rise—it is then that we become penetrable by the Spirit of God. As long as we imagine that the world can be changed by our activities, our good works, our energy, we substitute our effort for the power of God. That is as ineffective at it is blasphemous. 'For thine is the kingdom, the power ... ,' we pray, incidentally making a revealing and overlooked juxtaposition—and then, all too frequently, behave as if his is the Kingdom and ours is the power—and the glory too.

The power of God to transform, heal, renew and set free is grudgingly and half-heartedly accepted by most Christians at the personal level.

If we only half-believe that the power of God can change us, it is hardly surprising that we don't believe at all that it can change the politics of the world. And if we don't believe that, we are forced back either to total despair, or to fatalism—what will be, will be—or to hyperactivism.

By contrast, if we see prayer as a means of releasing God's power into the world, of enabling him to pour his transforming love into the critical centres of decision-making and activity, we begin to see paradoxically that we are not powerless at all. Our power to transform the world is God's power. That is hard to comprehend. Like so many spiritual truths, it is so simple that it takes some grasping. Certainly the mainline Churches have forgotten it or are afraid of it. I was asked to address the Synod of the Church of England on world development at the time of the publication of the Brandt Report. I concluded an analysis of the Report by saying that in my view, the proper response of the Church was one of, quite literally, prayer and fasting. Four days later I received an angry, stinging rebuke from a senior church official. 'I was very disappointed', he wrote, 'that all you could suggest was prayer. The last thing we want is to return to that kind of pietism …' When I enquired what help a major church-based charity gave its supporters to pray for the poor and the vulnerable, the answer was revealing: 'Oh God, we don't want people to think that all they've got to do is pray.'

Possible questions:

(a) 'As long as we imagine that the world can be changed by our activities, our good works, our energy …' What has your effort in following this course done for the Kingdom of God?

(b) What or who is Elliott referring to when he speaks of 'the critical centres of decision-making'? How do you think he sees God's 'transforming love' influencing these centres?

(c) What are the implications of this passage from Elliott's book for a Church leader heavily involved in organizing the activities of a community?

(d) Assess the validity of the argument presented in the third and fourth paragraphs of this passage.

The four short questions suggested do not look for recall of basic historical or theological *facts*; what they demand is, first, insight into the relation of God's love and forgiveness to man's exercise of power; and second, skill in expressing the relevant ideas and marshalling them into a connected argument. Instructions at the head of the examination paper would indicate that no answer should exceed (say) 300 words.

Activity 5: Research and discussion Select a suitable passage from a book and design a set of six questions of progressively increasing difficulty to test critical thinking.

Many institutions rely, for evidence of critical judgement, on essay-type examinations, and long essays or dissertations prepared by students as course work over a period of days or weeks. The great drawback of essay-type examinations is the force of institutional habit, the deep-rooted attachment of any institution to what has been done in the past. It is extremely difficult to change student perceptions of such examinations, or to persuade them that the examiner may not be primarily testing their knowledge of facts and accepted views. And it is equally difficult to persuade college staffs of the value of having agreed objectives and criteria in setting and marking such papers. Moreover essay-type examinations, when subjected to independent marking by several different examiners, or even successive markings by the same examiner, are demonstrably unreliable; that is they score low on consistency as between one examiner (or occasion) and another. They also place a high premium on speed of thought and fluency of writing; and the abstract wording of questions, added to the stressful situation, often cause candidates to misinterpret the questions altogether. There is also of course a large element of chance in the coincidence of a student's preparation with the questions actually offered.

Long essays or dissertations can also provide a useful test, but as already noted, they lend themselves to tedious reproduction of material from books and journals, as well as to unacknowledged collaboration between students. They are really only profitable when based on first-hand experience and detailed observation of people and situations, or on comparison and analysis of materials outside the standard repertoire, thus calling for a detailed interpretation of that material, which obliges students to engage in 'the intolerable wrestle with words and meanings'. There is no sharp dividing line between a 'long essay' reporting on a practical project or field-work investigation or job placement, and a piece of course work involving (say) comparative analysis of two authors' views on a controversial topic.

Tutors marking essays may find the following check-list of criteria useful. It runs parallel to the check-list suggested for students (p. 79) and the rating-scale suggested for use in distance learning tutorial work (p. 85).

(a) How far does the answer focus on the heart of the question, or is much of it irrelevant to that focus?

(b) Is the structure of the essay well-reasoned? Are problems posed and defined? Are possible solutions stated? Is evidence brought forward on these, and the solutions compared? Is a summary or conclusion presented? (The structure may be on other lines (see pp. 144–145), but similar questions must be asked.)

(c) How far has the student seen the wider significance of the topic under review? What signs are there of original ideas? Or is the essay pedestrian and descriptive, lacking in analysis?

(d) Is the weight given to different aspects of the subject proportionate to their importance?

(e) Is the language clear? Does it avoid long sentences and polysyllabic words except where indispensable?

> **Activity 6: Research and discussion** Get back three of your students' essays and mark them again in the light of these criteria. What differences in emphasis (if any) do you find between your original marks and the present ones?

The techniques of assessment for the higher order skills become especially significant where syndicate methods are used (see ch. 15). Any tutor who intends to introduce these methods must first make sure that all students realize that examinations of the types we have decribed will be a major component of the assessment procedure, leaving the knowledge of basic material and the grasp of the subject discipline to be tested separately. Students will need to be given ample practice in any new styles of examination.

NOTES ON ACTIVITIES

> **Activity 1** I would expect you to have said something to the effect that in setting tests of communication skills, examiners need to ensure that the questions really do test these skills. This would call for their definition, as written, oral, non-verbal etc. Examiners would need also to ensure that students do not expect the test to test anything else but those skills.
>
> **Activity 4** Here you would need to emphasize that if you tested a student's grasp of a subject discipline by an essay examination you would have no guarantee that a second examiner would award the students the same marks, nor that if you marked a script again a week later, the two marks would be the same.

19
Assessment techniques for professional objectives

ASSESSING EXISTENTIAL UNDERSTANDING AND PRACTICAL JUDGEMENT

As we have seen, Objective 9 reaches out into many fields of real-world study, practical judgement, practical skill and competence. We have looked at a wide range of both objectives and methods connected with the professional side of students' education, including:

(a) the organization of field work and job placements, involving detailed briefing, systematic de-briefing, and follow-up studies;

(b) the use of role-playing techniques for exploring human relationships and probing cultural assumptions;

(c) the use of case studies as a way of opening up an academic topic and of studying another culture;

(d) a variety of small-group techniques for getting students more fully involved in their studies and for developing critical judgement and team work skills;

(e) the use of drama, literature and film as ways of studying other cultures and promoting self-understanding.

All these educational techniques have among other purposes that of inter-weaving students' academic study with their real life activity and encouraging the fusion of ideas, concepts, principles derived from books and lectures and discussions with first-hand experience, whether of the world around them or of the world within. Many students will be working in situations where they are not only trying to connect academic material with practical experience but also acquiring 'tacit knowledge' of human situations and a practical judgement of other people's responses and their own proper action (see ch. 4). The question is, how do we assess the effectiveness of these techniques in achieving this fusion of the academic with the practical? How do we assess their success in developing students' tacit understanding of people and institutions and situations and communities?—or in developing their 'practical ability' to cope with everyday life and professional jobs?

> **Activity 1: Stop, think and note** Have you ever been assessed for practical judgement in dealing with people? If so, how did the assessor go about the job? Were you informed of the criteria by which you were to be judged? If you have not been so assessed, have you had to make an assessment of this sort for students in college? If so, how did you set about it?

These questions tend to be left unanswered by academic departments, or to be referred to professional bodies—whether colleges or organizations—concerned with standards of professional performance. This means defining the areas of professional performance—a task which can be carried out at very different levels of sophistication. At one extreme the criteria for students preparing for the ministry might include such requirements as:

(a) Successful application of the principles of pastoral care and counselling (e.g. in dealing with such problems as drunkenness and marital conflict).

(b) Successful practice of Christian education (e.g. teaching effectively in religious education classes in a local school).

But at a more sophisticated level we find the following formulation in a Church of England Report (102):

... The qualities [required] appear to be of three kinds:

1. Those by which the minister participates in the creative and redemptive activity of God through personal commitment to Jesus Christ in obedient faith; these demand an intelligent grasp, both intellectually and spiritually, of the fundamental features of this activity in the world as revealed in Scripture, tradition and Christian hope, and careful consideration of their practical implications.

2. Those by which the minister lives and works within and for the ministry of the whole people of God; these demand an intelligent grasp of the Church, its polity and life, and also the development of those interanimative abilities which are necessary for the building up of the ministry of the Church.

3. Those by which the minister identifies the situations to which the Church must address itself and brings the ministry of the whole people of God to fruition in them; these demand such informed knowledge of the affairs of the world, whether political, business, technological or social, as will enable full proclamation and realization of the creative and redemptive activity of God by which they achieve their proper being.

Such qualities can only be judged by experienced practitioners in each field, and the appraisal will inevitably be subjective. Nevertheless, steps can be taken to offset the bias involved in subjective judgements. The following guidelines suggested by C. C. Houle (103), though somewhat sketchy, may be useful:

1. Assessment should be made in real-life situations, preferably in the course of routine activities rather than in specially presented or 'staged' performances.

2. Several assessments should be made by different assessors on different occasions. The maximum range of evidence from varied sources is needed.

3. The dimensions of behaviour which assessors are to regard as most important need to be agreed in advance by the assessing body, and discussed and agreed with the students. These would need to include such qualities as those concerned with 'personal commitment to Jesus Christ in obedient faith'; a grasp of the way the Church—as the whole body of Christian believers—functions; practical skill in working with both ordained and lay people in specified situations; a grasp of the way the secular world functions in defined spheres; practical skills in working as a Christian minister in those spheres; and some degree of self-awareness and self-understanding. The list would be a long one, and would of course vary according to the region and the communities where the students were working.

Activity 2: Research and discussion Suggest twelve to fifteen personal qualities and skills or competencies for the list mentioned in guideline 3 above, bearing in mind the particular conditions and circumstances of your students.

---

4. The assessor team also needs to draw up schedules indicating standards of performance shown by students in the situations specified according to guideline 3 above. For example, a minister working with young people in a club or a school depends for his effectiveness on being able to establish good relations with the members, and a five-point scale of performance from A (excellent) to E (very weak; unacceptable) might take the following shape:

A: Has great natural capacity for finding the right wavelength for the club members or school pupils; readily evokes an enthusiastic response from them; adept at giving commendation or praise while setting demanding standards.

B: Gets on well with members or pupils; secures a positive response; gives due attention to individuals; commends good achievement, but is less successful in encouraging those who run into difficulties.

C: Gets on well with members or pupils, and usually pitches the activity or work at the right level; tries to give commendation to individuals, but at times abrupt and apparently unsympathetic to those in difficulties.

D: Has difficulty in making real contact with members or pupils; tends to speak over their heads; chooses illustrations outside their experience; gives little praise for good answers and merely rejects wrong answers.

E: Fails to make contact with members or pupils and is quite unprepared to follow up points made in their replies; reproves individuals for wrong answers.

Again, an important aspect of a Church leader's work is his self-evaluation and his response to advice, and a scale might be framed on the following lines.

A: Continually monitors own professional activity and relates the analysis to a general model; continually seeks advice; keen to discuss progress with senior staff; sufficiently confident to appreciate criticism and advice; self-critical and responsive to feedback from members or pupils.

B: Seeks advice; responds to suggestions; uses feedback from members or pupils; tends to follow advice without sufficient discrimination of the situation to which it applies.

C: Anxious about criticism from supervisors but usually accepts and acts on written criticism and advice; respects the experience of senior staff and their advice over management of club or class.

D: Makes little use of feedback; self-criticism becomes self-congratulation; insufficiently aware of own limitations; quarrelsome when actual performance discussed.

E: Rejects advice; tends to feel persecuted; quite oblivious of own limitations.

Activity 3: Research and discussion Draft a five-point scale for skill in leading a small group of lay Christians in some community activity.

In short, what has to be done by college staffs in assessment in this extensive field is to:

1. define in broad terms the qualities needed in a Church leader (as in the example quoted above);

2. list the practical skills and habits entailed by those qualities in the students' actual circumstances;

3. establish an assessment team who will draw up a procedure on roughly the lines indicated above;

4. call on the assessment team to define those features of the students' observable behaviour which may be regarded as constituting the occupational performance required;

5. call on the assessment team to draw up schedules of grading for those features of performance.

This may sound a straightforward procedure, but these are not simple exercises for assessors to settle in a few short meetings: rather, they are complex developments to be worked at gradually over the course of years.

ASSESSING EXPERIENTIAL LEARNING—PRE-ENTRY

Colleges sometimes also need to assess older candidates' previous experience and their reflection on this experience. Where candidates for admission are mainly school-leavers with standard qualifications, a college may not have adequate procedures for discovering the potential of older candidates who lack standard qualifications. The criteria by which staffs judge such candidates would probably include:

Basic literacy and numeracy;

Evidence of recent reading, radio listening, and television viewing on the subject;

Evidence of understanding what has been read, heard or viewed;

Evidence of ability to see the significance of first-hand experience;

Evidence of powers of communication, written or oral.

The usual method of appraisal is by essays and interviews. However, older candidates with scanty academic qualifications may suffer from a lack of self-confidence on first encountering an educational institution, and the usual essays and interviews may leave much good potential undisclosed. A more effective approach is to form a small class of such candidates, meeting over some period of time, so as to enable them gradually to build up a 'documented educational autobiography' (DEA). In this process they would learn to identify the different learning experiences they had undergone, and have the opportunity to bring forward examples of work previously undertaken, such as a memo written in the course of a job or a report of a discussion meeting. They would be able to review the knowledge and skills already acquired, gradually explore their relevant experiences and put them into words, and identify the people best able to vouch for their record. As before, a small assessment team should prepare guidelines for the selection procedure.

Activity 4: Stop, think and note Think of two older students whom you have known well. What experiences, knowledge or skills emerged during their time with you which were not uncovered at interview?

SELF-DIRECTED LEARNING, COMMUNICATION, AND TEAM-WORK SKILLS

Our discussion of the problems of assessment under Objective 9 presented certain principles which also apply to assessment under Objectives 3, 4 and 10. However, it may be useful to formulate some criteria for these, and the following are offered as practical suggestions.

Objective 3 (Self-directed learning)
Applying a three-point scale, the check-list in Rating Scale 2 may be useful.

Rating Scale 2: Self-directed Learning

This student:	True most of the time	True to some extent	Not true of this student
has pride in a job—takes a lot of trouble over it—is very conscious of the quality			
is methodical, thorough, persevering			
shows determination to get to the heart of a unit of study			
asks questions to extend under-standing and check knowledge/ takes initiative in seeking out solutions to problems			

Objective 4 (Communication skills)

Here we need to assess both face-to-face communication and written work. The criteria for competence in written work have been concisely expressed by an Examinations Council in England as follows (104):

> ... [Good language teaching] should train a 16-year-old secondary school [boy] to use the language confidently, appropriately and accurately, according to the circumstances in which it is used. He should be able to speak his own mind, to write what he has thought, and to have a care for the correctness of written and spoken English. He should be able to understand what he reads and hears, to master the ideas and re-state them in his own way. He should have some understanding of the different uses of language, of the language which relates, describes, evokes, persuades, and is the instrument of the creative imagination.

For written work the check-list in Rating Scale 3 may be useful.

Rating Scale 3: Communication Skills – Written work

This student:	True most of the time	True to some extent	Not true of this student
expresses ideas with precision			
expresses feelings and responses with precision			
uses short, direct words and sentences rather than long imprecise and involved ones			
gives evidence for views in a clear, logical way			
shows concern to select exact word, to convey sensitive discrimination			
adapts language to context: academic, politics, preaching			

Face-to-face communication, as in interviews or small-group work, involves more than the use of words, and much of the meaning is conveyed by non-verbal methods: facial expression, tone of voice, timing of responses. Much also depends on the way tutors listen: do we listen with sufficient care and attention to grasp a student's or candidate's opinion, or check back if we are not sure? As already noted (p. 88), the profitability of group discussion depends to a large extent on the climate of relationships in a group, and this in turn is strongly influenced by the tutor conducting the discussion. A sense of openness and mutual trust is likely to promote clearer and more sensitive communication, and helps to clarify obscurities and prevent mistaken interpretations of what people say.

Objective 10 (Team-work skills)

Obviously the team-work skills or competencies of Objective 10 overlap with those called for in face-to-face communication. Development under Objective 10 is probably best assessed in the same way as under Objective 9 (existential understanding and practical judgement): i.e. by experienced professionals observing students in real-life situations. For relationships in a group the check-list in Rating Scale 4 may be useful.

Rating Scale 4: Teamwork Skills

Relationships in a group This student:	True most of the time	True to some extent	Not true of this student
expresses self clearly			
talks too much			
talks too little			
co-ordinates discussion			
expresses appreciation of others' contributions			
expresses disagreement calmly			
accepts criticism without resentment			
Higher-order skills relates argument to evidence			
introduces new useful ideas			

introduces irrelevant material (a)			
clarifies part of discussion			
summarizes arguments			
questions shaky evidence			
adopts prejudiced position unsupported by evidence (b)			
recognizes main issue and challenges irrelevant ideas			
shows tolerance of others' views, concedes their validity			

Checklists of this sort can also include a contrasting negative contribution at each point on the list, such as those marked (a) and (b).

In the above rating schemes a three-point scale is used at some stages, a four- or five-point scale at others. College staffs will need to decide when and where to use such scales.

Activity 5: Research and discussion Draft a report for your college colleagues making recommendations as to where to use a five-point and where other scales in the assessments outlined in this chapter.

GETTING INSIDE CULTURAL ASSUMPTIONS

The great importance of Objective 11 was discussed at length in chapter 16. But it seems unlikely that the talent for 'getting inside other cultures' is generalizable. Most people's human understanding and sympathies are so heavily conditioned by their own culture and temperament. As with Objective 10, such a 'skill' or 'competence' can probably only be assessed by a small team of experienced professionals. In this case the students should perhaps be given a carefully chosen film, or short sequence from a film, where differences in perceptions and value assumptions can be traced. But the film selected would of necessity vary from one region of the world to another, and each institution would need to establish its own library of selected material and check-list of questions to be put to students.

As far as self-understanding is concerned, we should conceive assessment in terms of a team of experienced professionals, accustomed to working closely with students and seeing how they are coming to terms with their own strong and weak dispositions, and with their personal relationships, as well as with their life of prayer.

RELATIVE WEIGHTING OF ATTAINMENTS

At this point another important question arises: how do we balance all these Objectives against one another? What should be their relative weighting in the overall assessment of a student's attainment and promise?

At every stage there is room for considerable divergence of opinion and practice. In the purely academic sphere one well known educationist suggests that 25% of the total marks awarded in a final assessment should be assigned to Objective 1 (basic knowledge), 45% to Objective 2 (grasp of subject discipline), 20% to Objective 5 (application in new situations), and 10% to Objectives 6 (analysing an argument) and 8 (assessing quality). Some formal examinations in British universities set questions which in effect award 90–95% of the marks to Objectives 1 and 2; and this is undoubtedly the case in many countries.

The form of assessment varies similarly. In one British university 50% of the final total in one subject is awarded on the basis of a set of formal three-hour examinations, 30% to answers to previously announced questions and 20% to course work. In another subject 54% is allocated to a traditional examination, 13% to MCQ tests, 7% to a practical examination, 13% to a dissertation, and 13% to a project.

Any college staff, therefore, must at some stage study in detail the relative weighting to be given among Objectives 1, 2, 5, 6, 7 and 8— the range of knowledge and skills in the academic sphere—and then as between these more specifically academic aims and the rather diffuse Objectives 3, 4, 9, 10 and 11. Communication skills (Objective 4) are not usually assessed separately from academic achievement, since they are conceived chiefly as written communication; yet they are especially important for any Church leader. Objective 3 (self-directed learning) is largely a matter of personally developing a mature sense of responsibility, and is closely linked to certain aspects of attainment under Objectives 9, 10 and 11, while a major aspect of Objective 9 is development of the practical judgement of people and situations, often intuitive and based on tacit knowledge, which is vital to any Church leader. Similarly a major aspect of Objective 10 is sensitive skill both as member and as manager of a team. And finally Objective 11 refers both to understanding other cultures and to understanding oneself.

All these considerations suggest that any overall assessment of a student should take the form of a profile, perhaps on the lines of Rating Scale 5.

Rating Scale 5: Overall Assessment

	Five-point scale				
Objectives concerned with thinking	A	B	C	D	E
1. Basic knowledge 2. Grasp of subject discipline 5. Application in new situations/ problem-solving ability 6. Analysing an argument 7. Invention, originality 8. Assessing quality 4a.Written communication					
Objectives concerned with *professional competence*					

4b. Oral communication
  3. Self-directed learning
  9. Existential understanding and
    practical judgement
10. Team-work skills: participation
               management
11. Understanding other cultures
    Understanding oneself					

Qualities of personality Stability Dependability Integrity Drive etc. (Many further qualities and virtues could be listed here; every culture and every institution will need to compile its own list.)					

The mere listing of so many separate categories will, however, thrust experienced tutors back into their memories of all those individual students who have to them in real life been primarily *human persons*: who always remain in some sense unknown and mysterious. A system of categories like the above is essentially a tool for thinking and a tool for planning.

NOTE ON ACTIVITIES

Activity 5 In those areas of knowledge or competence that are of special importance for a student's future a five-point scale is desirable, since it discriminates more precisely between students of different capabilities. However, in some circumstances the difficulty of collecting a sufficient volume of observations and records may render a five-point scale impracticable; as for example with oral communication skills in real-world situations.

Appendix

As readers of this book will no doubt have recognized, a number of the educational techniques we have described represent fairly radical departures from the current organization, teaching style and assessment procedures in many colleges and university departments around the world. This means that those who would like to see these methods introduced in the colleges where they now teach would be wise to recognize also certain implications of the arguments we have presented. We shall therefore take a look at some possible strategies for bringing about any changes that may be decided upon, whether by a Principal, a Head of Department, an individual lecturer, or an Academic Board or Board of Governors.

COLLEGE CULTURE AND THE PROCESS OF CHANGE

Improvements in the field of education, as in most spheres of human activity, are brought about in different ways at different times and in different places. In the 19th century individual pioneers—the Swiss Froebel, the English Newman—would develop a fresh approach which others copied and disseminated. Since the first World War the orthodox and almost universal view has been that the correct, 'scientific', approach is to fund substantial experimental projects on a sufficient scale for new schemes to be tested in selected institutions on a strictly controlled basis. The pattern would be to set up parallel groups of students, one group to be taught by the customary and one by the experimental method. The students would be given standardized tests of knowledge or skill before and after the course; the conditions of the experiment and the intended results would be strictly defined. The results would be published, and those new schemes which showed good results would be made known by a central agency, through personal contacts at professional meetings, or through individuals looking for ways of solving their own classroom problems.

However, very large sums of money have been invested in such projects in different parts of the world to very little effect, and the consequent disillusionment of the educational world has led to a radical re-thinking of strategy. We have to go back to the concept of 'culture', on which so much emphasis has been laid in this book.

Every college has its own culture, its own web of habits, assumptions, ways of doing things, ways of seeing the job, and priorities among values; and various types of culture can be discerned in different institutions.

In a *power* culture the dominant influence is that of the head of the institution: decisions tend to be made at the top and passed down through the hierarchy. Such cultures are proud and strong. They have the ability to move quickly, and react well to threat or danger.

A *role* culture is assumed to work by logic and rationality: jobs and responsibilities are defined, procedures for communication prescribed, and decisions made by designated committees. Large organizations tend to operate in this way: a civil service, a Church with thousands, or millions, of members; a multi-national company. Such cultures are slow to change; there is a powerful inbuilt resistance.

A *task* culture is distinguished by emphasis on 'getting the job done', on bringing together the right people at the right levels with the right resources and letting them get on with it. Influence derives more from expertise than from position or personality, and so tends to be more widely dispersed than in a power or role culture. It is a team culture which makes use of the influence of a working group on its members, thus creating a bond of loyalty through which individuals tend to identify themselves with the institution as a whole, to believe in its objectives, and to reduce status differences. It tends therefore to be flexible and adaptable, since project teams can be quickly set up to handle specific problems, and dissolved when the problem is dealt with.

The latter two types of culture are not to be thought of as diminishing the authority of the head of the institution. As Douglas McGregor, the well known writer on business management, said on retiring from the presidency of a college:

> . . . I believed that a leader could operate successfully as a kind of adviser to his organization. I thought I could avoid being a 'boss' . . . I thought that maybe I could operate so that everyone would like me—that 'good human relations' would eliminate all discord and disagreement. I couldn't have been more wrong. It took a couple of years, but I finally began to realize that a leader cannot avoid the exercise of authority any more than he can avoid responsibility for what happens to his organization. (26)

Some theological colleges have a power culture, derived from their position in a large centrally-controlled Church organization and perhaps from a 'top-downwards' method of selecting college Principals and defining their job. Some have a role culture, with a strong committee structure, while in some there will be an element of task culture, with small project teams set up for handling specific problems.

Whatever the structure, the crucial factor in the effectiveness of the organization and the job satisfaction of the staff is *the degree of mutual confidence and trust pervading the organization*. This in turn depends on several factors. First is the extent to which the structure is happily acceptable to the people working in it. Some individuals are temperamentally uncomfortable in a power culture, others are uncomfortable if they are *not* in a power culture. Second is the way the head of the institution treats his colleagues. Do they feel that he values their contribution? that he is fundamentally honest and fair towards them? How far does he elicit their trust? When problems arise, how are they dealt with? Where are decisions made for academic policy? for community organization? How far are students involved in policy and administration? In a power culture, when members feel at home with decisions being made at the top, it is probably, in the late twentieth century, important that the person at the top should consult, and be known to listen attentively to, a range of people in the institution—those who are regarded as able to represent the general feelings and prevailing culture of the community.

In a role culture, where people are accustomed to having decisions made by duly constituted committees, careful attention needs to be given to the selection of committee members, and to ensuring the honest and fair working of the committees. When new proposals are put forward these need to be viewed as possible solutions to defined problems; in fact, such definition may be a major part of the 'problem'. Due care should also be taken to safeguard the position, both of those who implement a proposed change and those who oppose it.

Where a particular member of staff is responsible for the development of teaching methods, perhaps in charge of an 'Educational Development Service', this work should nevertheless be carried out largely on a consultancy basis: that is, by helping colleagues to sort out the classroom problems which they bring forward. As the American writer on business management, Edgar Schein, has so concisely put it,

> ... 'consultation involves the client and the consultant in a period of *joint* diagnosis ... The importance of joint diagnosis derives from the fact that the consultant can seldom learn enough about the organization to really know what a better course of action would be for that *particular group* of people with their *particular sets* of traditions, styles and personalities.'

A STRATEGY OF COLLEGE DEVELOPMENT

All this means that anyone, whether an individual lecturer, a departmental head or a Principal, who considers that techniques suggested in this book would be useful in a particular college, will need to estimate first how far such techniques will fit in with the general culture of the college and its sponsoring body, with its assessment procedures, and with the cultures or sub-cultures of relevant groups of staff and students. Staff unconvinced of the wisdom of any new approach brought in are often found to be misinterpreting or misapplying it. Students are not only extremely sensitive to any change which may appear to threaten their examination results, but take a very long time—possibly years—to change their perceptions and expectations of assessment techniques unless special steps are taken to help them both to understand and to practise a new system.

Even at the level of Principal, and in a situation that appears favourable, it is advisable to prepare the ground of any change with care. Whatever the pattern of organization in a college, the staff can only be expected to give of their best if they are operating the methods they use from a basis of understanding and conviction. That is, whether they are happy to try out a new approach or prefer to adhere to their customary methods, they need to be clear about the values underlying the alternatives, and the priorities they assign to these values. And the Principal needs both to safeguard the position of the conscientious conservative and give support to a lecturer wishing to try new ways. If new methods are adopted without adequate understanding and at least provisional commitment they are unlikely to be successful. Any Principal, therefore, who wishes to launch some rethinking of teaching methods will almost certainly find it advisable to set up some kind of working group or groups, with carefully composed membership and terms of reference, to consider possible changes.

And even where the situation is most favourable, a junior member of staff hoping to introduce any change will certainly need to prepare the ground very carefully indeed. In most colleges probably the first thing to do is to approach one's immediately senior staff-member with a written proposal, explaining the change suggested and the reasons why it appears desirable. (This latter point is almost always most profitably presented in terms of handling some recognized or recurrent problem in the college.) Having thus secured some support and advice on tactics, the next step may be to approach the college Principal or Vice-Principal for similar understanding and support. In some colleges the Principal will have power to decide upon implementation; in others the agreement and backing of a committee or academic decision-making body may be needed. Once a decision for implementation is given, the next step will be to explain the proposal to any colleagues who may be affected by the scheme, and then do the same for the students. Where any change concerns the assessment pattern, it is essential to give students advance practice in the new style, including trials under examination conditions, so that they not only understand the new pattern clearly but have full confidence in the system and in the staff who administer it. If the scheme is fairly ambitious and elaborate, a small steering committee might be formed to keep an eye on it.

Since the teaching load of staff in many colleges is heavy, and the preparation of new schemes inevitably time-consuming, it is usually important, especially where the weight of conservative opinion is powerful, to move slowly, finding a small number of volunteers to try fresh approaches. Some procedure—and time—should also be built in for evaluation of the new work, getting feedback from both colleagues and students.

In some situations, college Principals sharing, say, a university or denominational affiliation and within reasonable distance of each other, might find it worthwhile to adopt an 'Action Learning' approach, as outlined in chapters 4 and 10. Three or four Principals could form a small consortium, each specifying a problem in their college teaching programme and appointing a senior, respected staff member to act as 'Consultant Fellow' to one of the other colleges for (say) three months. Each Principal would give sufficient access to information and facilities to enable the visiting Fellow to carry out enquiries and formulate proposals. The Fellows would also visit the other three or four co-operating colleges, thus helping one another in their tasks. Some allowance for temporary replacement staff in each college would be needed, and probably a small steering committee to supervise the project. Such a project would, however, only be practicable if there was a rather high degree of mutual trust and confidence within and between the colleges, as well as the necessary finance for staff replacements, travel etc.

GLOSSARY

Action Learning: A technique used in training industrial managers, in which a group of managers learn from a co-operative study, and the effective solving, of actual management problems; hence, any method of professional training based on the co-operative handling of real problems.

Advance Organizer: A question or brief report clearly based on what is already known but which sets students' minds working on a fresh topic about to be started.

Associative Group Discussion (AGD): A technique in which the first part of a discussion session consists of an exercise carried out by members individually, providing an experience on which the ensuing discussion is based.

Basic Christian (or Ecclesial) communities: Small groups of people who meet to study the Christian faith and to work together in its light for the benefit of their community.

Buzz groups: Groups of three or four members formed within a lecture audience to discuss a specific topic for a few minutes.

Critical judgement: Competence in analysing and assessing the validity of a statement or argument.

Culture: The web or fabric of customs, meanings, relationships and values which characterize any given society, community or organization.

Debriefing: The stage at the end of a practical project when the various aspects of the exercise are reviewed and assessed.

Deep processing: An active approach to study, which involves searching out the inner core of the argument in a given document, and looking for any personal relevance or meaning in it.

Distance Learning: An adaptation of Open Learning for students located at a considerable distance from their study centre.

Espoused theories: Theories about human situations and actions acquired from academic sources.

Existential understanding: To say that one has an 'existential' understanding of a given idea means that in some sense one's grasp of it 'goes beyond' a purely 'intellectual' or 'theoretical' grasp and exerts a strong influence on one's feelings, judgements and/or decisions. The phrase may be interpreted in metaphorical terms by saying that the idea has become 'part of one's mental furniture', or that one 'feels it in one's bones'.

EXPERIENTIAL LEARNING: Knowledge and skills acquired through being directly in touch with the realities being studied.

MODIFIED ESSAY QUESTION (MEQ): An examination question in which a case study or report is presented and a series of questions posed on it requiring perhaps 50 words for each answer.

MULTIPLE CHOICE QUESTIONS (MCQ): Short questions, each of which offers several possible answers from which the candidate has to choose one as correct.

OBJECTIVES: The purposes to be achieved in a course, defined in terms of what a student will be able to do, rather than know or say, as a result of the course.

OPEN LEARNING: A system of study designed for students who cannot attend the usual timetabled sessions in an educational centre, and who therefore study in isolation.

PRACTICAL JUDGEMENT: The phrase is used to refer to a judgement, usually of people and human situations, which is not worked out by a process of explicit logical thinking, but arrived at without being put into words, 'intuitively'.

PROFILES OF ATTAINMENT: A record of a student's performance which summarizes the levels attained in academic knowledge, intellectual skills and other forms of competence, together with an indication of certain personal qualities.

PYRAMID TECHNIQUE: A technique in which a lecturer asks students to consider a specific question for two minutes; then asks them to form pairs and consider what methods could be used for handling the problem posed; and finally asks them to form groups of four to consider which of these methods would be best for the problem set. The groups of four then report to the class.

RATING SCALES: A technique for analysing a student's performance by offering a list of different aspects of that performance and asking the examiner to award an assessment for each, on a given scale. This is usually a three-point scale (e.g. 'high', 'average', 'low') or five-point (e.g. 'outstanding', 'superior', 'competent', 'weak', 'fail').

RELIABILITY OF ASSESSMENT METHOD: An examination paper is said to have a high reliability when it yields the same marks when given to the same class on different occasions, or when marked by different examiners.

ROLE PLAYING: A technique for enabling students to explore personal responses to given situations, by acting out the various specific roles in those situations.

SURFACE PROCESSING: An approach to study in which a student tends to concentrate on memorizing unrelated facts or ideas.

SYNDICATE METHODS: A technique in which a class is divided into groups of 5–8 students who work as small teams on assignments set by the tutor, and produce reports on their findings.

TACIT KNOWLEDGE: Knowledge, especially of people and human situations, which cannot be fully put into words; intuitive knowledge.

THEORIES-IN-USE: In contrast to 'espoused theories', 'theories-in-use' are the theories implied by the actions people actually perform.

VALIDITY OF ASSESSMENT METHOD: An assessment method is said to have high validity when it does in fact measure achievement in the knowledge, skill or competence which it was intended to measure.

VALUES: Commonly used in various senses. Here (p. 34) it means those objects, conditions of living, or ways of behaving on which people set a value or which they regard as important, not so much as part of their conscious intentions as of the underlying driving forces or aspirations of their lives.

Further Reading

Chapter 1
1. Kinsler, F.R., *The Extension Movement in Theological Education.* 2nd edn, Pasadena USA, William Carey Library, 1981.
2. Kinsler, F.R., ed., *Ministry by the People.* Maryknoll USA, Orbis Books, 1983.
3. Hogarth, J., Gatimu, K. and Barrett, D., *Theological Education in Context.* Nairobi, Uzima Press, 1983.
4. Winter, R.D., ed., *Theological Education by Extension.* Pasadena USA, William Carey Library, 1969.

Chapter 2
5. Whitehead, A.N., *The Aims of Education*, London, Williams and Norgate, 1929.
6. Newman, John Henry, *The Idea of a University*, Discourse VI. 1853, 1858.
7. Freire, P., *Pedagogy of the Oppressed.* Harmondsworth UK, Penguin, 1972.
8. Bloom, B.S., ed., *Taxonomy of Educational Objectives I: Cognitive Domain.* New York, McKay, 1956.
9. Further Education Unit (FEU) of the British Department of Education and Science (DES), *Curriculum Styles and Strategies.* 1982. Also other practical reports.
10. The Business and Technician Education Council (BTEC) of Britain, *Common Skills and Core Themes: General Guidelines.* 1986.
11. BTEC, *Common Skills and Core Themes: Illustrative Material and Advice.* Also other useful documents.

Chapter 3
12. Squires, G., ed., *Breadth and Depth.* London, Nuffield Foundation, 1976.
13. Marton, F., Hounsell, D. and Entwistle, N., eds, *The Experience of Learning.* Edinburgh, Scottish Academic Press, 1984.
14. Entwistle, N., *Styles of Learning and Teaching.* New York, Wiley, 1981.

Chapter 4

On tacit knowledge:

15. Greenleaf, W.H., *Oakeshott's Philosophical Politics*. London, Longman, 1966.
16. Polanyi, M., *The Study of Man*. London, Routledge and Kegan Paul, 1959.
17. Heaton, E.W., *The Hebrew Kingdom*. London, Oxford University Press, 1968.

On the relation of academic knowledge to 'real life':

18. Schon, D.A., *The Reflective Practitioner: how Professionals think in Action*. London, Temple Smith, 1983.
19. Burgess, T., ed., *Education for Capability*. Windsor UK, NFER-Nelson, 1986.
20. Chickering, A.W. and Associates, eds., *The Modern American College*. San Francisco, Jossey-Bass.

See also (1), (2).

On Action Learning:

21. Revans, R.W., *Action Learning*. London, Blond and Briggs, 1980.

On Church and politics:

22. Temple, William, *Christianity and Social Order*. Harmondsworth UK, Penguin, 1935.
23. Newbigin, Lesslie, *Foolishness to the Greeks*. London, SPCK, 1986.
24. Elliott, Charles, *Praying the Kingdom*. London, Darton, Longman and Todd, 1985.

See also (6), (7).

Chapter 5

25. Mackenzie, N., Eraut, M. and Jones, H.G., *Teaching and Learning: an Introduction to New Methods*. Paris, UNESCO, 1970.
26. McGregor, D., *The Human Side of Enterprise*. London, McGraw-Hill, 1960.
27. Collier, G., ed., *The Management of Peer-Group Learning*. Guildford UK, SRHE, 1983.
28. Handy, C.B., *Understanding Organizations*. 3rd edn, Harmondsworth UK, Penguin, 1985.

Chapter 6

29. Krass, A.C. *Go ... and make disciples* TEF Study Guide 9. London, SPCK, 1974.
30. Donovan, V.J., *Christianity Rediscovered*. 2nd edn, London, SCM Press, 1982.

31. Harrison, R., 'Understanding your organization's character' *Harvard Business Review*, May–June 1972.
32. Shaw, G.B., *Saint Joan*, Constable, London, 1924.
   On the technological outlook in industrial societies:
33. Cotgrove, S., *Catastrophe or cornucopia*. Chichester UK, Wiley, 1982.
   On 'espoused theories' and 'theories-in-use':
34. Argyris, C. and Schon, D.A., *Theory in Practice: Increasing Professional Effectiveness*. San Francisco, Jossey-Bass, 1974.
35. Song, C.S., *Tell us our Names*. Maryknoll USA, Orbis Books, 1984.

Chapter 7
36. Rudd, E., *A new look at postgraduate failure*. Guildford UK, Society for Research into Higher Education (SRHE), 1985.
37. Rudduck, J., *Learning through small-group discussion*. Guildford UK, SRHE, 1978.
   On Open Learning and Distance Learning:
38. Coffey, J., *Development of an Open Learning system in Further Education*. London, Council for Educational Technology (CET), 1978.
39. Lewis, R., *How to develop and manage an Open Learning scheme*. London, CET, 1985.
40. BTEC, *Implementing Open Learning*. 1987.
41. Taylor, Harold, *Tend my sheep* TEF Study Guide 19. London, SPCK, 1983.
   See also (9), (28).

Chapter 8
42. Hargreaves, John, *A Guide to I Corinthians* TEF Study Guide 17. London, SPCK, 1978.
43. Filochowski, J. and others, *Reflections on Puebla*. London, Catholic Institute for International Relations, 1980.
44. Clark, F., *Luther and Lutheranism*. Milton Keynes, UK. Open University Press, 1972.
   On problem-based learning:
45. Boud, D., ed., *Problem-based Learning in Education for the Professions*. Sydney, Australia, HERDSA, 1985.
   See also (19).
   On audio-visual aids:
46. Flood-Page, C. and Kitching, J.B., *Technical Aids to Teaching in Higher Education*. 3rd edn, Guildford UK, SRHE, 1981.
47. Saunders, D.J., *Visual Communication Handbook*. London, Lutterworth Education, 1979.
   See also (20), (25).

On defining objectives:
48. Beard, R.M., Healy, F.G. and Holloway, P.J., *Objectives in Higher Education*. Guildford UK, SRHE, 1974. See also (9).
On published self-study materials:
49. Hiscox, R., *Eager to Learn*. London, Church House, 1986.

Chapter 9
On the design of TEE courses at post-primary level:
50. Battey, R., *TEC Syllabus Writers: Instructor's Manual*. London, CET, 1979. See also (1), (2), (3), (4).
51. Moyo, J. and Holland, G., *Bringing People to Jesus*. Kisumu Kenya. Evangel Press, 1973.
52. Simalenga, J., *What is the Bible?* Nairobi, Organization of African Instituted Churches, (OAIC), 1985.
53. Batlle, R., *How Jesus sees Women*. Nairobi, OAIC, 1987.
On contextualization:
54. Davies, J.D., *Beginning now*. London, Collins, 1971.
55. Boff, L. and C., *Introducing Liberation Theology*. London, Burns and Oates, 1987.
56. Gutiérrez, G., *A Theology of Liberation*. London, SCM Press, 1974.
57. Gitari, D.M. and Benson, G.P., *Witnessing to the Living God in Contemporary Africa*. Africa Theological Fraternity, 1986.
58. Dickson, Kwesi A., *Theology in Africa*. London, Darton Longman and Todd, 1984.
59. Koyama, Kosuke, *Water Buffalo Theology*. London, SCM Press, 1974. See also (3), (4), (7), (23), (30).
On training in prayer:
60. Teresa of Avila, *Autobiography*. Harmondsworth UK, Penguin, 1957.
61. — *Interior Castle*. London, Sheed and Ward, 1946.
62. Quoist, M., *Prayers of Life*. Dublin, Gill, 1963.
63. Fosdick, H.E., *The Meaning of Prayer*. 29th edn, London, Collins, 1954.
64. Gibbard, M., *Why Pray?* London, SCM Press, 1970.
On Bible Study:
65. Weber, H-R., *Experiments in Bible Study*. Geneva, WCC, 1981.
66. Wink, W., *Transforming Bible Study*. London, SCM Press, 1980.

Chapter 10

On the organization of practical schemes:

67. Adderley, K. and others, *Project Methods in Higher Education.* Guildford UK, SRHE, 1975.
68. Walter, G.A. and Marks, S.E., *Experiential Learning and Change.* Chichester UK, Wiley, 1986.
See also (10), (11).
On role playing:
69. Milroy, E., *Role-Play: a Practical Guide.* Oxford, Pergamon, 1982.
On prayer:
70. Küng, Hans, *On Being a Christian* (Glasgow, Collins 1978), pp. 432–5.

Chapter 11

71. Miller, C.M.L. and Parlett, M., *Up to the Mark.* Guildford UK, SRHE, 1974.
On tutoring:
72. Lewis, R., *How to tutor in an Open Learning Scheme.* London, CET, 1981.
73. FEU, *Tutoring.* London, DES, 1982.

Chapter 12

74. Abercrombie, M.L.J. and Terry, P.M., *Talking to Learn.* Guildford UK, SRHE, 1978.
75. Sheldrake, P. and Berry, S., *Looking at Innovation.* Windsor UK, National Foundation for Educational Research, 1975.
On the management of discussion groups:
76. Bligh, D., ed., *Teach thinking by discussion.* Guildford UK, SRHE, 1986.
77. Abercrombie, M.L.J., *Aims and Techniques of Group Discussion.* 4th edn, Guildford UK, SRHE, 1978.
78. Jaques, D., *Learning in Groups.* London, Croom Helm, 1984.
79. Cockburn, B. and Ross, A., *Teaching in Higher Education* (series of nine booklets). Lancaster, University of Lancaster, 1980.
See also (20), (37).

Chapter 13

On memorization:

80. Baddeley, A., *Your Memory: a User's Guide.* Harmondsworth UK, Penguin, 1982.
81. Hunter, I.M.L., *Memory.* Penguin, 1955. Now out of print.
82. Hinson, D.F., *The Books of the Old Testament* TEF Study Guide 10. London, SPCK, 1974.
See also (14).

Chapter 14
83. Parlett, M. and Simons, H., *Learning from Learners*. London, Nuffield Foundation, 1976.
84. Highet, G., *The Art of Teaching*. New York, Knopf, 1950.
On the use of audio-visual aids see (46), (47).
On the preparation of lectures and explanations:
85. Brown, G., *Lecturing and explaining*. London, Methuen, 1978.
86. Bligh, D., *What's the use of lectures?* Harmondsworth UK, Penguin, 1971.
87. Manchester Polytechnic, *Designs for Teaching: Lessons and Lectures*. London, CET, 1979.
88. Gibbs, G., Habeshaw, T. and Habeshaw, S., *53 Interesting Things to do in Lectures*. Bristol UK, Standing Conference on Educational Development Services in Polytechnics, 1985.
See also (79). This chapter is much indebted to (85) and (88).

Chapter 15
On syndicate methods in practice see (27), (76).
On the overall influence of group work see (19), (20).

Chapter 16
89. Poulton, J., *The Feast of Life*. Geneva, WCC, 1982.
90. Torres, S. and Fabella, V., eds, *The Emergent Gospel*, Maryknoll USA, Orbis Books, 1984 (quoted in Parratt, J., *A Reader in African Christian Theology* TEF Study Guide 23. London, SPCK, 1987).
91. St John of the Cross, *The Dark Night* Book 2.
92. Ngugi Wa Thiong'o, *The River Between*. London, Heinemann, 1965.
On the organization of practical projects and role-play see (67), (68), (69).
On the use of drama, novels and films:
93. Schwab, J.J., *College Curriculum and Student Protest*. London, Chicago University Press, 1969.
94. Collier, G., Wilson, J. and Tomlinson, P., eds, *Values and Moral Development in Higher Education*. London, Croom Helm, 1974.

Chapter 17
95. Rogers, C., *On Becoming a Person*. Boston USA, Houghton Mifflin, 1961.
96. Maslow, A.H., *Toward a Psychology of Being*. New York, Van Nostrand, 1962.

Chapter 18
97. Rowntree, D., *Assessing Students: How shall we Know Them?* London, Harper and Row, 1977.
98. Macintosh, H., Nuttall, D. and Clift, P., *Measuring Learning Outcomes.* Milton Keynes UK, Open University Press, 1981.
99. Klug, B., ed., *A Question of degree.* London, Nuffield Foundation, 1975.
100. Deale, R.N., *Assessment and Testing in the Secondary School.* London, Evans and Methuen, 1975.
101. Hinson, D.F., *History of Israel* TEF Study Guide 7. London, SPCK, 1973.
See also (9), (29), (50), (79).

Chapter 19
102. Advisory Council for the Church's Ministry, *Report of the Working Party on Assessment.* London, Church House Westminster, 1985.
103. Houle, C.C., *Continuing Learning in the Professions.* San Francisco, Jossey-Bass, 1980.
On principles and methods in these areas see (9), (10), (11), (76), (78), (97), (98), (99).
On the assessment of pre-entry learning:
104. Evans, N., *Curriculum Opportunity.* London, DES for FEU, 1983.
105. *A Language for Life.* London, HM Stationery Office, 1975.
On rating scales see (9), (10), (11), (97), (98) and (99).
Appendix
On college cultures and the process of change see (28).
On strategies of institutional development:
106. Hewton, E., *Rethinking Educational Change.* Guildford UK, SRHE, 1982.
107. Boud, D. and McDonald, R., *Educational Development through Consultancy.* Guildford UK, SRHE, 1981.
See also (28), (79).

ADDRESSES

The following are the addresses of the organizations mentioned in the Further Reading list:

BTEC: Business and Technician Education Council, Central House, Upper Woburn Place, London WC1H 0HH

CIIR: Catholic Institute for International Relations, 1 Cambridge Terrace, London NW1

Church House: Church House Publishing, Church House, Dean's Yard, London SW1P 3EZ

CET: Council for Educational Technology, 3 Devonshire Street, London W1N 2BA

FEU: Further Education Unit, Elizabeth House, York Road, London SE1 7PH. Publications from: Publication Despatch Centre, Department of Education and Science (DES), Honeypot Lane, Canons Park, Stanmore HA7 1AZ

HERDSA: Higher Education Research and Development Society of Australasia, c/o Tertiary Education Research Centre, PO Box 1, Kensington, New South Wales 2033, Australia

Nuffield Foundation: The Nuffield Foundation, Nuffield Lodge, Regent's Park, London NW1 9PS

NFER: National Foundation for Educational Research, Darville House, 2 Oxford Road East, Windsor, Berks. SL4 1DF

OAIC: Organization of African Instituted Churches, PO Box 21736, Nairobi, Kenya

SCEDSIP: Standing Conference on Educational Development Services in Polytechnics, c/o Centre for Educational Services, Bristol Polytechnic, Coldharbour Lane, Bristol BS16 1OY

SRHE: Society for Research into Higher Education, at University of Surrey, Guildford, Surrey GU2 5XH

WCC: World Council of Churches, 150 Route de Ferney, 1211 Geneva 20, Switzerland

Index

This combined index covers the main subjects dealt with, and includes the names of people mentioned or quoted in the text. An asterisk indicates that a subject appears in the Glossary.